These People Are Not Your Friends

Jason Lye

Copyright © 2016 Jason Lye
All rights reserved.

These People Are Not Your Friends
The complete works available in print for the first time,
comprising The Dark Art of Staff Management and Facts of Life
for Managers.

These People Are Not Your Friends: the Dark Art of Staff
Management © Jason Lye 2012.

These People Are Still Not Your Friends: Facts of Life for
Managers © Jason Lye 2015.

This book is sold subject to the condition that it shall not, by
way of trade or otherwise, be lent, resold, hired out, or otherwise
circulated without the author's prior consent in any form of
binding or cover other than that in which it is published and
without a similar condition, including this condition, being
imposed on the subsequent purchaser.

Jason Lye has asserted their moral rights to be identified as the
author of this work.

ISBN-13: 978-1518808104
ISBN-10: 1518808107

First published as two bestselling e-books

These People Are Not Your Friends:
the Dark Art of Staff Management
© Jason Lye 2012

and

These People Are Still Not Your Friends:
Facts of Life for Managers
© Jason Lye 2015

JASON LYE

For anyone I've ever worked with

CONTENTS

Titles are Vanity, Perception is Sanity 9

Part I: The Dark Art of Staff Management 13

It's all about you 15

Let's meet the teams 21

Beating out an MBA 26

Evolution through devolution 32

Hating can be motivating 37

It's OK to be a control freak 42

Slapping down pointless enthusiasm 47

Random acts of malevolence 51

Momentary lapses of cool 54

How to win at meetings 58

Hell is other people: surviving team building events 61

Encouraging a resignation 65

You cannot trust HR 70

Recruitment: Satan's bingo 76

These people are not your family 80

Part II: The Facts of Life 85

Growing up is hard to do 87

You can run away from difficult questions 91

You can't avoid the occasional humiliation,
so brace yourself   94

Sometimes you are forced to report to a nutter   100

Talking rubbish is a useful skill   109

Undermining is bad (unless you're forced into it)   115

Walk like a man, talk like a Mandarin   121

Your team will occasionally make your life
a living hell   125

Management is teal and other nonsense   130

No good deed goes unpunished   136

You will spend a lot of time baffled   139

Dealing with idiots is an everyday thing   144

The United Nations of hell   151

Hocum locum – being the Outsider   156

Board games: what to expect when you're on
a senior team   159

There's always a bigger fool than you   164

COMING TO TERMS WITH YOUR DESTINY   169

10 ways to really screw up as a manager   172

Six books to read over a stiff drink   174

Acknowledgements   175

About the author   176

TITLES ARE VANITY, PERCEPTION IS SANITY

Welcome to the world of management. You may have got here through your own entrepreneurialism, through promotion or by landing a job you're not quite sure yet that you can pull off. However you got here, you are now operating in a whole new world in which you are now company royalty.

You may still be basking in the afterglow that your new title brings. You may indeed still be sneaking smug looks at your new business card just to see it in print. It's said that the right job title provides status and self-esteem; that people really care about their job titles and will sometimes even choose the better title over more pay. Doesn't it fill you with pride when you tell people that you are now a Manager? Or, better still, a Director? Isn't there a reason you've got this title? Isn't it because you're better than everyone else? Well isn't it?

There is an insatiable appetite everywhere for titles and status. Some are obviously open to abuse: Erection Engineer was recently voted the worst job title of all time, beating Knob Head (transportation, since you ask) and District Beaver Leader for the title. But if you are reading this book, the chances are that you will be called something much grander, possibly something preceded by the word "Head". Rest assured that someone somewhere will already have christened your title something very different from the one printed on your business card. The word "Head" may still feature, but it is likely to be itself preceded by the word "Pin". Or "Dick". Or, indeed, "Knob".

The point is that your title is relevant only to your ego and, until they find a way to manipulate it into something embarrassing, to the lucky herd of people who now look to you as their boss.

To your own bosses and/or shareholders, you are simply a buffer between the great unwashed and them; something to soak up the buffeting of constant demands for better working hours, more pay, bigger bonuses, petty backstabbing and playground squabbling. In more difficult circumstances they will expect you to be their Rottweiler. It's true that there is no "I" in "team", but then again "team" is an anagram of "meat". That's how your management views your team and, for that matter, you. Either way, you are now sandwich filling.

If you have made it up through the ranks, you will at least understand what needs to happen in order to get the job done. The aim now is to get people to do it for you. If, on the other hand, you have been appointed to a management position from elsewhere, you will have quickly twigged that you need to conceal your ignorance at all costs – what we in the business call managing "blind". Whatever route you took to get here, and whatever you might have done along the way, the need to develop some outstanding management skills is both critical and urgent.

You could invest in a course in management theory or read some of the millions of books that outline the psychology of teams, leadership skills and techniques that you should master if you are to become the model manager. But then again, why bother? These books paint dangerous pictures of a future in which it is possible to become an in-control and popular manager of a team of well-motivated, shiny happy people. This, as any seasoned manager will tell you, is unachievable and will only serve to demotivate you to a state of permanent gloom. Is this what you want?

Management is not a science; it is a dark art founded on finely-tuned skills of illusion, manipulation and sleight of wit. This book will show you how to develop those skills, by explaining key aspects of management that need to be mastered to achieve the perception of success – and hence protect your own longevity. Use it wisely.

PART I

The Dark Art of Staff Management

IT'S ALL ABOUT YOU

"If this were a dictatorship it'd be a heck of a lot easier, just so long as I'm the dictator"
George W Bush

The most successful managers learn early that they need to divert the energy they had previously put in to the job that got them promoted in the first place. They quickly realise it's no longer about the business or the company, it's about them. Treat your own career as a job, and put all your energy into it. Your job is now you.

One of the most common mistakes made by inexperienced managers is to assume that they have the support of their staff. That has to be earned or, more effectively, instilled using the variety of tactics described in this book.

While you will be keen to get to know your new team, you can be sure that they will regard your arrival as nothing but an opportunity to settle some old scores and get some longstanding whinging off their chests in the guise of "feedback". You may also have been charged by your own managers to identify the strengths and weaknesses of the people who now work for you. As if they didn't already know. Be under no illusion that this will be a largely pointless task to keep you occupied and off their list of things to worry about for a while.

Here's what to look for when introducing yourself in your new role.

First of all, if you've been set a pointless task by your boss, ignore it. Work out what's in your own best interest and do that first. You're clever enough to work out how to present something to your managers later.

Secondly, don't think your team is ever going to regard you with anything better than benign wariness. That's the best you can hope for, especially after a pay review or the first time you are forced to discipline one of them. These people are not your friends, as they will eventually show you. They will smell blood at a "nice guy" image. David Maister, previously of Harvard Business School, advises managers to ask themselves what, precisely, they want to be famous for. Nowhere is this more relevant than in deciding your own management image. Decide now on what kind of reputation you want to have with your staff, then walk in tomorrow and start building it.

If you have been promoted to head up a team you were once part of, then you will need to negotiate an additional fundamental obstacle: doing things to them that had previously been done to you. Your ambitions aside, you are now at the sharp end of any unpleasantness that your own management want to inflict on the little people. In addition to whatever title they have used to flatter you into submission, you are their instrument of destruction: the bad cop to their good cop, their disciplinarian and chief executioner. You will need to develop the tightrope walking skills of the entire Cirque de Soleil to deal with this one.

Not so long ago, an acquaintance was promoted to management, realising too late that he was expected immediately to assume the position of executioner and cull half of his new team. On the plus side, this immediately instils a fearsome image that can be used to great advantage later (see Random Acts of Malevolence). On the flip side, he never got the chance to use it, being dispensed with himself shortly thereafter.

Every day your counterparts in every other company on earth are being forced to implement pointless rules and systems, the only effect of which is to attract the disdain of the team whilst providing no obvious benefit to the business. In this situation an Oscar-worthy performance is necessary when you profess that you too think it is a good idea.

Let's say that one of your charges decides that the company should instigate "dress-down Wednesdays", and mobilises support from others to petition you to the point where you begin to harbour dark thoughts, some very dark thoughts. Some types of business preclude this kind of informality, which gives you a rule or a business standard behind which to hide. But if you're in a business where your staff never go out, never see customers, or are never seen by the outside world, why not? But then what do you do if your boss has inexplicably strong feelings against casual clothing when you don't really care either way? Can you be bothered to fight your management for something as trivial as this? Or the alternative: can you face the constant chipping away of your underlings as they become ever more militant in their desire to wear their spangly hotpants to work on a Wednesday?

See what I meant when I said you are now sandwich filling?

You could always defend your boss's stance on the matter through a convincing act that you too believe that people think better when well-dressed. But if you decide to fight for the team on this one, and if your boss bows to popular demand, then be under no illusion that he or she will expect something from you, personally, in return. You will have taken one for the team – make sure they know it.

This is all part of realising that you must now choose whether you run with the hounds or with the fox – and even if you do now run with the hounds, you are still their bitch.

In short, forget about popularity. The best you can hope for is to pull it off without inciting mutiny in your team or long-standing hatred in any individual victim. In the words of PG Wodehouse, "I could see that, if not actually disgruntled, he was far from being gruntled". If your team is less than gruntled most of the time, that's worthy of a big pat on the back for you. Granted, it's aiming low – but at least it's achievable so that's one SMART objective under your belt right there. Those management books that cynically imply that you can have it all – the effortless control, the happy band of permanently dedicated and motivated workers – are dangerous. You can't.

But while your team may be functioning on low levels of "gruntle", you don't have to. And, anyway, it's all about you.

Choosing your style: the "fourth way"

It is said that a good leader inspires people to have confidence in the leader, but that a great leader inspires people to have confidence in themselves. It is also said that you should never give a sucker an even break. Finding your management style involves somehow reconciling these two conflicting truisms.

When you walk into your office as a new manager, you will already have given some thought to the kind of management style you want to adopt. You may even have read those books that tell you to decide what kind of person you want to be seen as, then act it out. The problem with this approach is that you will find it impossible to keep up the appearance of a dynamic yet sensitive although somehow hard-assed individual for longer than the five minutes it will take your new staff to find see right through your act. You need to find a style that will enable you to pull the wool over their eyes without the need for RADA training.

The most widely accepted styles of leadership are what I call "the three -tions":

1. **Instruction**
"You will do this."
The choice of authoritarian regimes the world over.

2. Suggestion

"You may wish to consider the benefits of doing things this way."

Typically found in the Diplomatic Service, politics and conversations involving the most sinister baddies from the world of James Bond movies. Note, however, that this does not work with the typical team because managing by "hint" like this goes right over their heads.

3. Emotion

"By doing this you will change someone's life."

Most frequently found in the Charity sector (where it is often true) and in global terrorism (where changing someone's life is an accidental byproduct of crazy actions by stupid people).

But why should you have to choose between the Chinese government, Blofeld and ISIS as role models? If you've made it this far, you should be able to combine all three in a fourth, much more effective approach.

4. Prediction

"If you don't do this, there will be consequences."

This approach can be made to fit literally every situation you will ever face, and can be delivered amicably or fearsomely, depending on your mood.

JUST REMEMBER

Pretty much any management style is tolerated as long as you are consistent.

In the same way that airline safety demonstrations tell you to put on your own oxygen mask before helping others, put your own sanity before anyone else's.

LET'S MEET THE TEAMS

"The botanist is he who can affix similar names to similar vegetables, and different names to different ones, so as to be intelligible to everyone."
Carolus Linnaeus, the Father of Taxonomy, whose system
for naming, ranking, and classifying organisms is
still in use today

Whether you are new to the company, or promoted from within, it will be important in the early days and weeks to understand the battlefield ahead of you. Here's what to look for when meeting your team. A simple categorisation will help you enormously as you shimmy up the greasy pole.

All staff fall into one of three categories: Greenhorns, Politicians and Cardigans. You may not think so at first but rest assured that the more experienced you get, the more this makes sense. Amuse yourself by creating your own categorisations.

Category 1. The Greenhorn

This may be a new or inexperienced person or, alternatively, a more established member of the team who has never quite "got it", but who remains enthusiastic. The latter is more difficult to deal with, but similar management principles apply.

An ambitious Greenhorn, of whatever age and ability, will often give every appearance of having understood the task you have set for them. Sadly, they will later prove that they didn't understand a word. The trick is to differentiate between the Greenhorns who "get it" and those who never will.

The Greenhorns who just don't "get it" will eventually evolve into Cardigans (see Category 3).

But occasionally, very occasionally, you will uncover a Greenhorn who has an innate understanding of your business and their role within it and who, delightfully, combines this understanding with an impressive competence in getting their job done. A diamond in the rough. Nurture these people to the point where they are doing your job for you, yet are still sufficiently low-level to accept your superior position rather than attempt to leapfrog you in the hierarchy. Maintain this status quo for as long as you can through a combination of praise and begging (to your management, for regular buckets of liquid cash in the form of salary increases and bonuses for them).

But avoid holding them up as a paragon of virtue to others in your team: that will only create resentment and unleash the office dogs of war onto your second most valuable asset — the first being your own rear end (see later). Company history is riddled with examples of situations where a senior manager has PR-ed an employee to others, usually without their consent or, indeed, knowledge, leading to good people feeling unaccepted, lonely and somehow victimised just for doing a blindingly good job.

When the inevitable happens, and your diamond sparkles so brightly that you can no longer hide the light from your management, you need to be in a position where the diamond feels they owe you their career. If they are going to leapfrog you, make damn sure they don't jump too low. To modernise an old adage, be nice to those on their way up: you will need them on your way down.

Category 2. The Politician

This is someone who is clearly going places, often someone with no natural ability for the job but who will one day be more successful than you will ever be.

The trick with the Politician is to spot him or her early. With luck and a little wit you can match them up with a sideways move, preferably into someone else's team, at the earliest possible opportunity.

Category 3. The Cardigan

Age has no bearing on the Cardigan. This is someone who has settled comfortably into their job and their place in the team. They are usually nothing less than competent; unfortunately, they will never be any more than that either.

Nothing you can say or do will have any effect on the Cardigan, so there is no point in wasting too much time on them when so many others are demanding your attention.

The actor Peter O'Toole was once asked why he was wearing two watches at the same time, as he often did. "Life is too short," he replied, "to risk wasting precious seconds glancing at the wrong wrist."

However, Cardigans are sometimes the glue that binds a team together, to the extent that some, however misguidedly, like to think they are the life and soul of any party going on. I call these the "Partygans". In that respect, they may be fulfilling a useful role so, when you catch yourself equating "Cardigan" with "slave", it's best to make sure that you are a benign master. Many Cardigans are also very well acquainted with employment law and tribunals are best avoided.

The Politicians and Greenhorns will try their hardest to bleed you dry emotionally and spiritually. They will cynically leave behind a dry husk of what used to be a decent person and a competent worker: you. And it's a sad truth that, if you stick around long enough, everyone will leave you in the end. The best thing you can do is to be as humane as you possibly can be to the Greenhorns, Politicians, Cardigans and any other categories you uncover. But never forget that these people are not your friends.

A WORD IN YOUR REAR

It is often said of managers that some have problems distinguishing between two important parts of their anatomy, one of them being the elbow. Your elbow is mostly harmless, and of little relevance to your management position. Your rear end, on the other hand, is your most prized asset. Although you may find yourself speaking through it from time to time, the true purpose of your rear end is to be bared and whipped when things go wrong. So make sure it's covered at all times.

Your management role and your rear end are co-dependent. If you want to look after both, you will need to remember the three most important rules of management. Even the dimmest student on day 1 of a business studies degree should be able to remember this one. It is, of course, documentation, documentation, documentation.

So, in all dealings with your staff, document early and often. History is written by the victors: if you write the history, then it's only logical that you will come out the victor.

JUST REMEMBER

By all means categorise the people in your team. Find out what drives each individual, then use that information to help them and you.

Treat everyone with the same attitude and general manner. If you have favourites, hide the fact - from them and everyone else.

BEATING OUT AN MBA

Beware the Jabberwock my son!
The jaws that bite, the claws that catch!
Beware the Jubjub bird, and shun
The frumious Bandersnatch!
Lewis Carroll, Jaberwocky

It is possible that you have inherited, or inadvertently employed, someone with an MBA. Does this inoculate them against the inevitability of developing the characteristics of any of the three categories described in the previous chapter? Of course not. They will already have a natural tendency towards one of them. The overriding aim here is to keep them out of harm's way while you figure out how to offload them without anyone noticing.

One of the first things that you'll discover on hiring an MBA newbie is that they will truly believe that they know more about your business than you. Don't bother to argue the basics of your business with them: you'll find that argument is not only futile but also dangerous to your health. Remember that they have been trained in business by highly-qualified academics.

Ask yourself this. How many MBAs have created successful businesses themselves? Compare that with how many of them end up in parts of businesses created by others that have different – or no – letters after their name. It's no secret that an MBA is commonly nicknamed by entrepreneurs as a Master of Bugger-All.

All MBAs are fluent in Jargonese, since this is the language in which an MBA is taught. Jargon is a term used in linguistics to describe the meaningless babble of one-year-olds just before they learn how to talk. They copy the sounds and cadences of the language being spoken around them but have no idea of what it means. To the older listener, jargon is incoherent, nonsensical and meaningless although, coming from a baby, undeniably cute. You can already see the parallels with MBA-type baby talk.

Outside the classroom, translation of Jargonese into English takes up time that can be better spent making money for the company. Jargonese is anti-business. It is your duty to your company, not to mention the English language, to stamp it out. Management consultants have tried hard to help in this process. In 2003, Deloitte Consulting unveiled "Bullfighter", a software programme which identifies jargon in documents. "We hope that it is a fun way to make business communications safer for all of us," they declared, before adding: "We envision a centre of excellence where our accelerated change agents can maximise their core competencies."

Of course, Jargonese is sometimes spoken by other, less gloriously-qualified staff too – they use it to disguise the fact that they don't know what's going on. The same rules apply. If they can't learn English, get rid of them.

If you want a Master of Bugger-All to engage usefully in your business, then it will be necessary first to wipe out anything related to their MBA. As they will have spent time (sometimes a whole two years) and a great deal of money on becoming qualified business experts, this will require all the qualities of guile and cunning that got you to a management position in the first place. This is your advantage.

The guiding principle with an MBA newbie reflects that of the underlying principle of medicine: first, do no harm; second, do some good. While you figure out whether they are ever going to be able to do some good, put them in a position where they cannot harm you or, worse, irritate you to the point where you harm them. The last thing you want is to spend hours chewing over endless theoretical flights of fancy and jargon that sap your time and energy but which, paradoxically, is the very thing that will energise and motivate them.

If you work for a large corporation that is awash with cash, then you can easily sideline the MBA into a role where he or she cannot interrupt the good thing you have going in your department. Have them think of a project that, while pointless in the extreme, keeps them away from your well-oiled machine while giving you some insights or information that you can use to impress your own management. This will buy you time while you watch and judge whether the MBA will ever be able to adjust to being a useful member of staff.

If the MBA is bright enough, as they should be, to realise that business revolves around pragmatism, drudgery and the kind of creativity that has a practical benefit somewhere, then graciously grant them entry into your inner circle. You may have a diamond on your hands.

If, however, your MBA clings to theoretical principles and jargon; if they fail to get to grips with the everyday grind that is the job, then they are highly likely to fall into the category of Politician. You then have a dilemma on your hands. You cannot afford to be stuck with them. Yet you cannot have your own boss think that you are not capable of developing someone with a bright mind (well, they have an MBA don't they?).

Your only choice is to big them up: point to their masterful use of words like "stakeholder", "leverage" and "strategic imperatives", and make your fellow managers believe that they are a star in the making. With any luck they will be poached in double-quick time. Or, failing that, they will come to believe that they are too good for your team and seek employment elsewhere. Either way you can take heart from your increasingly well-honed skills of manipulation in getting the result that you want.

If you've been unlucky or foolishly optimistic, and have realised too late that you have employed this latter category in a company that you yourself own, then there is no time to waste. These people will never understand why they cannot contribute to your business. They will also want your money. If you've missed the opportunity to get rid of them early, then the only option is to play on their ego and make it clear that your company will never fly high enough for them. Bore them to the point of resignation (and instruct a friendly recruitment consultant to find them another job).

Understanding Jargonese

Is leadership the same thing as management? Why are strategic imperatives so important to stakeholder strategy? These are the kinds of question on which MBA students have been trained to debate ad nauseam. When the manager sets out his vision for the team and then manipulates them into delivering it, is that leadership or management? Similarly, does anyone really know what they mean when they say they "have a strategy"? Why do people argue so much about whether something is called a "strategy" or an "objective"? Does it matter? Why does anyone care?

Here is a brief glossary of terms commonly found in Jargonese, together with their translation into English:

Leadership. Persuading people to do things they really don't want to do.

Management. Making sure that everyone works as hard as they possibly can, or preferably harder, for as little money as your company can get away with.

Market access. Gaining entry to Portobello Road, Petticoat Lane or any other street blocked for days by stalls selling knitted stuff you'll never need. Alternatively the bus to Billingsgate fish market, Smithfield meat market or, in fact, any market regardless of whether it is selling fish or meat.

Market drivers. Men in white vans who deliver stuff to and from markets and who sometimes smell of fish or meat as a result.

Objectives. The opposite of subjectives.

Penetration. You will know what this is, but MBA students often need to be reminded that two people need to be present for penetration to occur.

Planning strategically. What you have to do in order to generate a "strategic plan" (see below).

Strategic drivers. Men in white vans who smell of fish or meat but – and this is important - who have twigged that, to make money, they need to be delivering fish or meat to people who actually want it.

Strategic imperatives. No-one knows what this means.

Strategic plan. The end result of "planning strategically" (see above).

Strategy. Not tactics. And not objectives either.

Stakeholders. Van Helsing's little helpers.

Tactics. Tic-Tacs for dyslexic people.

Targets. Your staff.

JUST REMEMBER

People with MBAs often have a theoretical approach to things that can be frustrating, particularly in the year after having completed their MBA. However, they will know things that you can use or adapt.

Be firm when culling a course of action that is of no practical value, and don't be afraid to cut time-consuming theoretical debate if it is not contributing anything to the task.

EVOLUTION THROUGH DEVOLUTION

"Evolution has no foresight and does not plan for the future."
Nick Lane, *Life Ascending*

It is part of the expectation of any manager that they encourage and develop their staff, and so evolve their team into ever-higher-performing beings. But how to encourage these other species without having your own die out? In other words, how much work can you offload onto others while making sure that you remain useful enough to avoid redundancy when recession kicks in and the axe begins to swing?

First, let's look at evolving your team. In his brilliant book *Life Ascending*, Nick Lane describes how life originated in hot vents at the bottom of the ocean, then went on to evolve into the wonderful panoply of living organisms that we see today. This is exactly the sort of thinking that the clever manager should adopt in ensuring the evolution of the people working for him or her. Put them in a well-ventilated office and blow hot air at them occasionally. Most will equilibrate in a natural and stable state of spirit-sapping bottom-feeding. But the most successful species will rise to the surface and crawl out of the ocean to become sophisticated creatures in their own right, helped on their way by the odd pearl of wisdom from you.

Of course, the pearls of wisdom you deliver will never be the ones that they remember. What they remember will be all sorts of other things you've said. Every now and again, they will interpret some throwaway comment you've made in quite an insightful way – make sure you jot this down and add it to your ever-growing necklace of pearls so that you can stun others with it later.

Training is often regarded by most staff members and some companies as necessary for successful evolution of the individual. Others class it alongside whiny requests for stratospheric pay rises and increased holiday entitlements in the "ridiculous demands" category. "You can't ask me to do this – I haven't been trained" is a common cry from the Greenhorn. Note that this demand will never relate to a task for which a training course actually exists. No, it will always relate directly to the job they should be doing – and have, more to the point, been employed to do. Tread carefully with these people – these will be the cute ones who study employment law in their spare time and will not hesitate to complain to your boss that it's your fault they don't know what they are doing.

If it's not safe to tell them they have to learn on the job, as it were, then you have no choice but to make up a Heath-Robinson arrangement of spurious "training" tasks and grit your teeth as you watch them waste time when they could be doing something useful.

Most textbooks or management guides will refer to the distribution of work to your team as delegation. I prefer to think of it as "devolution", because "delegation" leaves you lumbered with both the responsibility and the risk that you will have to rescue a half-done job at the last minute. The last thing you need is delegated work regurgitated in your direction: it will by then be an unrecognisable hash which will hit you as a nasty mess and, just to make it a hundred times worse, right on top of the deadline. If you make it clear that you have a policy of devolution, the work goes to the individual along with the burden of responsibility – and if they fail in their responsibility you can take whatever disciplinary measures entertain you best.

Devolution of tasks to your team differs between businesses in terms of how best to achieve it, and is realistically far beyond the scope of this – or any – book. Devolution of responsibility, on the other hand, is a different matter and one that allows you to duck difficult situations with ease. At a company of my acquaintance, a team bonding event held at a hotel near London's Heathrow airport resulted in a form of team co-operation that was not only unfortunate but also very public. Happily for us, it provides an excellent illustration of how an embarrassing situation can easily be made someone else's problem.

The episode in question involved the bonding of two staff members far too closely in the hotel swimming pool.

As luck would have it, the pool was furnished with underwater windows enabling those sitting in the bar on the next level down to view the action – with reactions from spectators ranging from disgust to downright envy. Did the senior manager deal with it? Of course not. He collared the line manager of one of them and made her do it first thing on Monday morning.

Incidentally, the same company set up an "Employee Appreciation Day", on which every member of staff was given a mug bearing the "Employee Appreciation Day" logo. The message was clear: if you work here, you're a mug. Try keeping a straight face while explaining that one away to your team.

Another company event I attended attracted a letter of complaint that "The whole thing was carried out with a complete lack of aplomb." Make sure that you're not in charge of aplomb at these events – it's too risky if things go wrong, and you can still take the credit if it's a storming success.

Now, how to conjure up a widespread perception of your own value having offloaded all of the difficult and boring tasks to others? Taking the credit for a job well done is basic stuff, and you will already have mastered this skill. You will also have worked out that, however capable your team is, you must keep the most glorious tasks for yourself.

A holiday provides an unbeatable opportunity for showing how valuable you are. Having booked your two weeks in Honolulu to recharge your batteries (after all, you are now very busy and important), let it be known that you don't want to be disturbed. Just be sure to engineer one small issue to arise shortly before you are due to return.

Make sure that this one thing is something to which only you could possibly know the answer. This sends a message to all of the team, and to your boss, that you are totally indispensable to the company.

Growing new strains of life in the petri dish of the office calls for PhD-level management chemistry. A continuous drip-feed of devolution will help your team evolve and create the perception of personal development for your staff, but be careful to balance this with healthy dollops of reminders of your own importance if you want to keep your own species alive.

JUST REMEMBER

Delegating responsibility for a task gets better results than simply delegating the mechanics of the process.

Remember to keep your own profile high by showing that you too are delivering on your own tasks.

HATING CAN BE MOTIVATING

"As I trickled white paint from one end of [his] car to the other I could have danced with pleasure. Finally, I pinned his boxer shorts to the aerial."
Lady Sarah Graham-Moon, wronged wife

If a manager could have a superpower, what would it be? Invisibility? No, you're only going to hear things about yourself that you won't like. Flight? No point. Much more useful is the power of hate: that most driving and motivating of forces; the force that is so hard to control that it erupts in flashes of intense heat or supercools over months or even years into the icy permafrost of revenge.

For several years, Dashiell Hammett, author of hard-boiled detective stories including *The Maltese Falcon* and *The Thin Man*, lived, drank and fought with playwright Lillian Hellman. During one of their drink-fuelled bouts of raging aggression, a furious Hellman suddenly noticed Hammett grinding a burning cigarette into his cheek. "What are you doing?" she cried. "Keeping myself," replied Hammett, "from doing it to you."

If only he had learned how to harness the power of hate.

One thing they will never teach you at Harvard is *hativation*: the skill of using hate for good. It's OK to experience momentary flashes of hatred for your staff. You're only human. And on the plus side it brings your competitive nature into play – and competition is good, isn't it? Even if you don't think of yourself as particularly competitive, who's the one with the flashy title and the executive chair? Exactly.

One of the dark arts of management is to manage your own negative feelings and target them to people and areas where they can do most good.

There are two kinds of hatred that you will experience in management. The first is a general hatred of all humanity, where you begin to think of your team not in terms of the individuals it comprises but as a single multi-legged mutant: ugly, not viable outside the confines of the office, and useless. The second kind involves flashes of hatred triggered by specific acts or traits of individual staff.

If you are experiencing a period of general hatred, take the opportunity to practise your management skills on the team. So what if some neat trick that you've read about in some management self-help guide doesn't work? Who cares? Not you, and probably not them either.

Moments of specific hatred are very different. Every manager, at some point in his life, has an "I can't quite believe you did that" moment when someone they have nurtured and encouraged, and in whom they have invested a lot of emotional energy, does something so fantastically disloyal that it's hard to forget, let alone forgive.

Here's some advice for you. If the betraying party is useful to you then hate them as much as you like in your spare time but never, ever, let them see it at work. Just make them work harder than they have ever worked in their sneaky, two-timing little life. Drive them to the point of exhaustion, all the time lauding their value to you and to the company. Load on the responsibility to your heart's content. After a while you will find that not only have you managed to offload half of your workload but, by not rising to the betrayal, you have created a strong impression that you have much more important, interesting and fun things to do.

Even though you may be secretly seething several years later, you will wake up one morning to the realisation that you are the one with the life, the profile and the moral high ground, while they are the one with the wrinkles, the hair loss and the reputation of "a good do-er, but not management material". That moment of realisation will be one of the most satisfying of your life.

Other things that inspire hatred of a specific individual often stem from things that, in all fairness, you can do nothing about – the way they slurp their tea, for example, or some irritating mannerism you've noticed. There is no alternative but to live with these minor irritations.

However, if someone has been stupid enough to attract the laser beam of your hatred by doing something they should not have done; if they have cocked-up in a sufficiently wilful, obvious and clear-cut fashion as to warrant punishment, then by all means let rip.

It's said that you should praise in public but punish in private. Fine, but make sure that the punishment is loud and capable of being easily overheard by the rest of your earwigging team. Even Tom Peters, champion of motivational leadership, acknowledges that punishment is an art form and recommends that the errant employee should be threatened to within an inch of his life.

You will feel much better after this, and the flash of hatred will die away. Just don't go and spoil it all afterwards by trying to be nice.

FIVE WAYS TO MOTIVATE YOUR TEAM

You do not need any training to motivate a team. Just follow the five basic principles below and you will not go far wrong.

Care

Show you care, by keeping a log of every mistake they make. Then use it.

Respect

Don't try to be their friend. It is more important to be respected than liked. But it is more satisfying to be feared than respected.

Appreciation

Say thank you, but in a very sarcastic way, preferably after they have really cocked up.

Management

Practice MBWA - Management By Wearing Away. Grind them into submission. Or crush them. Up to you.

Partnership

Create a feeling of partnership with your team by trusting them with challenging projects. In other words, delegate well (ie. keep the peachy jobs for yourself).

JUST REMEMBER

If someone has given you just cause to be annoyed, calmly point out what they have done and what they can do to atone for it. Then let it drop.

If you have developed an irrational aversion to some quality or trait of an individual, you will need to find a way to live with it. You are not alone.

IT'S OK TO BE A CONTROL FREAK

"Now at least I know where he is."
Queen Alexandra on the death of her husband,
Edward VII

In his ragbag of random, office-related banalities *The Pursuit of WOW!*, Tom Peters lists various tips for keeping staff fresh, happy, and doing a great job, presumably with the ultimate aim of having them so motivated that they don't need management. Perhaps you would like to try out some of these with your own team.

First, says Peters, try calling "time out". "Hey beancounter, why not take the accounting department team to the movies this afternoon? Or to see one of the members' kids perform in a play?" He then recommends MBDA: "Management by Donuting Around". Apparently there is no better investment in staff renewal than doughnuts, muffins and balloons, and managers should set up a "crazy money" fund which gives everyone access to $25 for a spur-of-the-moment bagel or pizza party.

While it's true that Peters was writing for that parallel universe known as the United States, let's take a minute to imagine what would happen in the typical British office. Not having to work for the afternoon: happy. Having to watch *Hot Tub Time Machine 2*, the only film playing at a sensible time in your local cinema: *not* happy. And who in their right minds would willingly go and watch anyone else's kids in a school play? That's just crazy talk. The only staff renewal that could possibly result from this kind of stupidity is the need to recruit new Greenhorns as the current team, spooked by your behaviour, back carefully out of the room and into new jobs.

Speaking of crazy, you will have by now have thought of several alternatives for MBDA. Steer well clear of this madness unless you want Donut-brain, Muffin the Mule, BagelBastard, BollockBreath, or variations thereof, for a nickname.

If you want to get in control, and stay in control, then it is of paramount importance that you avoid acts of such cloying tackiness. It does not fit the fearsome image you are trying to build. At best, staff see right through it and despise you for patronising them from such a great height; at worst, they are confused by your sudden unpredictability. Once won, control must be maintained at all costs – not by motivation but by imposition, and by intervention and manipulation at every conceivable opportunity.

Hands-off management will eventually get you into trouble. If being a control freak means that you do it right, and if you care about doing it right, then control freakery is for you.

If you are a natural control freak, then move right on to the next chapter, or write to Jason@notyourfriends.com and contribute to the next issue of this book. If, however, you lack the confidence to take control, are in the early days of a management job, or just find it hard to care what your team is up to, then read on.

Think back to when you were a small child. Whenever you did anything you knew you shouldn't, how come your mother always knew? She even knew if you were just thinking about getting up to no good. How did she do that? Maybe you should have asked because this is something you now need to learn. Control freakery is made possible by guilt: not yours, of course, but the natural guilt latent in most people. It is on this that the pure control freak lives and thrives.

I knew of a company owner with a compulsive and constant itch to know what his employees were up to at all times. He refused to countenance the fitting of partitions in the vast, echo-y office space and installed himself headmaster style at one end, his desk facing across the office floor so that every single member of staff was in his line of sight. The staff secretly called him "The Invigilator". It was the quietest office in the world.

Not satisfied with simply being able to see and hear everything, he had to be restrained by his partners from inspecting staff emails for no good reason, and rumour had it that he had once had emails removed from the inbox of a fellow director without anyone knowing. But whether or not he was regularly snooping on the affairs of others, the general view was that it was the kind of thing he would do. This is genius. On the basis of rumour alone, he managed to prevent staff not only from forwarding sarcastic emails among themselves, but also from having any natural interaction between each other, thus successfully stifling any blossoming dissent without actually doing anything at all.

The best control freaks manage successfully to combine this play on guilt with techniques that keep their team constantly off balance. They want their staff insecure in their abilities with all judgement gone. Then they move in for the kill. Here's how to do it.

If you assign a task to someone, every now and again drop everything and make sure you respond to something before they have had a chance to do so. This is a classic technique for making someone feel somehow inadequate while at the same time showing that you have "overachiever" tendencies – and that has to be good. So flood your team with early-morning emails, and solve the occasional problem before your employees have a chance to come up with something themselves.

If, despite your best efforts, someone still appears too happy and relaxed for your liking, subject their work to a period of unnecessarily close inspection. Find fault with it. Let your petty side run riot. Let's say someone has written a report. Even if it's perfectly written and clear as a bell, find something to misunderstand. Pick on a section or paragraph and ask them to communicate it in a way that's less confusing. Once they've done that, tell them "it's still not quite there" and have them do it again. Or turn your attention to the punctuation: you need only to point out a few missed commas and minor typos to have them panicking that you have serious concerns about their attention to detail. Without having issued a single significant criticism, you now have them chasing their tails in a vicious and ever more panicky circle as they try and find the result that pleases you.

Once they have stopped thinking straight, you are at liberty to impose your will in whatever way you like. You now have control.

JUST REMEMBER

Ensuring good quality work is not control freakery.

It can be a fine line between control freakery and bullying. Self-awareness is vital for the manager with these tendencies but ironically this quality tends to be lacking in such people. Find a lieutenant whose judgment you respect and allow them to tell you if you are acting strangely.

SLAPPING DOWN POINTLESS ENTHUSIASM

"I will not make an issue of this campaign. I am not going to exploit, for political purposes, my opponent's youth and inexperience."
Ronald Reagan

One day, someone will come to you and say "Hey Your Majesty (or however you have decided to term yourself): I've had a great idea! Let's all bring a bottle of wine into work on Friday, knock off an hour early and have a Wine Club! That would be a fantastic way of encouraging team bonding."

Your inner sarcasm immediately fights back with: "Yes, let's all get drunk on office premises while our transatlantic clients are still phoning and expecting us to meet the most important deadline of the week." You could actually say that. But you will quickly gain a reputation for smothering enthusiasm that will make your team more difficult to manage, and which might make it back to your boss.

How do you deal with this type of misguided enthusiasm while still remaining popular?

The simple answer is to let them do it – once. Then use your ingenuity and knowledge of other team members to make sure it fails. Using the example above have the perky Greenhorn, for it is always the Greenhorns who have the silliest ideas, bring in a bottle of wine and open it in the main office area while the Cardigans and Politicians are struggling to meet the deadlines that you have cunningly set them a few days beforehand. Then sit back and fight the impulse to look smug as the Greenhorn with the bottle of Tesco's Lambrusco waits forlornly for the first person to appear for "bonding". It won't happen. Understanding your team means knowing that it means more for them to finish their work and disappear home or to the pub than to support one of their own in a venture they don't benefit from enough.

Having sanctioned the idea as an experiment, you are in the clear and can watch with satisfaction as it slowly dawns on the Greenhorn that their great idea is destined to fail.

Margaret Thatcher once famously said that "there is no such thing as Society". In the same vein, there is no such thing as a Team when the chips are down and people have their own individual desires at heart. It's a small victory for you, but a highly encouraging example of how isolating a particular individual can temporarily destroy the integrity of a team and help you stay in control while still appearing to be the good guy.

This is a great example of ensuring failure and consequent alienation of the naïvely enthusiastic young offender (also known as "*falienation*"), one of two techniques you might find helpful in such circumstances. The other is, of course, impedance. If you can't be sure of engineering a situation where such stupid ideas will fail, then the best course of action is to throw obstacles in the way until the Greenhorn's flash of enthusiasm dies away. Generally this does not take long.

Using the example above, let's say that you have a team of functioning alcoholics that would happily sell their grandmothers for a go on a £4.99 bottle of Poundstretcher's own-brand Chardonnay, especially on a Friday afternoon. You cannot be confident that "falienating" the individual will work.

When the Greenhorn comes to you with his great idea, tell him that company policy is to escalate all such requests for activity on office premises for discussion by senior management. Then make him fill in a form. A long and complicated one. Invent one if you have to. Once completed, file it out of sight for a few weeks, then confess that you asked him to complete the wrong form. Tell him that what he completed was a request for a single-occurrence event; what he should, in fact, have completed was a request for a recurring event. Invent another form and have him fill that in. When, several weeks later, you let him know that his request has been denied, chances are he will no longer care – and may even have forgotten about it entirely.

Adopting these two simple approaches will protect you from accidentally sanctioning anything that your own bosses may disagree with, while also saving you from having to suffer cringeworthy and contrived events such as this. Don't, whatever you do, suggest an alternative event off-premises in an attempt to show that you are not a killjoy. They will let you pay for it all, you won't be able to claim it back on expenses, and you will have lost an evening of your life to a group of people who will never even know what the inside of your house looks like.

JUST REMEMBER

If you can allow your team to make a harmless mistake without getting into trouble yourself, then let them do it.

If you cannot risk a mistake being made, and if you cannot point to a hard reason why a stupid idea will not work, then by all means be creative in preventing it from happening.

RANDOM ACTS OF MALEVOLENCE

"Nobody expects the Spanish Inquisition! Amongst our weaponry are such diverse elements as: fear, surprise, ruthless efficiency, an almost fanatical devotion to the Pope, and nice red uniforms…"
Monty Python

While the best approach to management is consistency, the best way of control is unpredictability.

Management by mood swing is a good approach but one that works only for a subsection of the management population and, if thoughtlessly done, can take on a whiff of harassment that is difficult to defend in tribunals. Unless you are a woman of menopausal age, this is a difficult one to pull off. However, if you are a woman hurtling towards the menopause (or can present yourself as such), then this is one of the few things that you can legitimately use to your advantage.

Much more effective for most managers is the random act of malevolence.

Former tabloid editor – and later, key phone hacking witness - Kelvin "The Frenzy" MacKenzie once sent his staff a joke Christmas gift: a piece of bread for toasting. When it popped up from the toaster, the bread bore a message: "Hit your sales targets next year or you're toast!" The combination of surprise, threat and timing makes this a true classic of its genre.

Disgraced, and now deceased, media mogul Robert Maxwell was a true professional in inventing new ways to invoke fear among his employees. Maxwell kept his staff in a constant state of terror. A BBC News report records an incident involving a journalist who was working at his desk when he felt a sharp blow to the back of his head. Turning round, he was horrified to see Maxwell looming over him. Maxwell peered at his victim. "Oh," he said, before walking away. "Mistaken identity."

Famously, a man who enraged him by smoking in a lift was sacked on the spot, with a £250 pay-off thrust into his hand by Maxwell to send him on his way. It was only later that Maxwell found out the man was not in fact one of his employees, but a courier who had been delivering a package to the building.

Gordon Brown, on the other hand, got it completely wrong. In a now long-forgotten exposé, a nation coughed nervously as it lapped up the media reports of Britain's Prime Minister pushing secretaries off their chairs, grabbing staff by the lapels, regularly throwing things around the office and, quite splendidly, bullying the head of an anti-bullying charity out of her job. But can you spot his elementary mistake? Of course you can. These acts, while threatening and possibly quite well timed, lacked the vital element of surprise. If you let this approach become the norm, it will lose its magic. You will have committed the ultimate sin of predictability. And you will look very childish. Unless you're in politics you can do much, much better than this.

Of course, random acts of malevolence need not involve any physical activity. Sharp wit and sarcasm, especially when uncalled for, can have an equally terrifying effect, especially when delivered with a helpful smile. Take the following exchange to which I was party just the other day:

Writer: "Does anyone know anything about the kidneys? Any idea where they are?"

Boss (smiling): "Would it help if I punched you in them?"

Fabulous comedy all round; the writer somehow feels a little bit threatened, but it was so obviously a joke — wasn't it? — that he can't complain. And the exasperated boss descends a few notes on the scale of frustration that can eventually culminate in a momentary lapse of cool (see next chapter). Everyone's a winner.

JUST REMEMBER

Aim for consistency in approach at all times but...

If you cannot resist a random act of malevolence, think about how you can incorporate humour to help defuse its effects.

MOMENTARY LAPSES OF COOL

"If you can't surprise the enemy, it is better to surprise your own side than no-one at all."
1st Gurkhas subaltern, Francis Hughes

Despite your best efforts at being grown up, you are occasionally going to blow your cover.

The American writer and humourist Joe Queenan once visited an anger management therapist to discuss his tendency to scream at inconsiderate mobile phone users. "I understand," the therapist said. "But what you need to think about is not what they are doing but what your needs are in that situation. What is it that you hope to get out of the situation?" "My needs are for them to shut the hell up," Queenan replied. "What I need to get out of the situation is take the phone and ram it down their throat!"

However inappropriate you think the Queenan approach is, there will be times when you find yourself using it.

As with most things that are dangerous to your health, prevention is better than cure. Even Queenan would probably agree that it's best not to lose your cool in the workplace when you are the boss. Avoid all human contact when you feel the anger rising, and take yourself well away from the shop floor. If you've got your own office, stomp into it and shut the door. Let them all think you're brooding – the retribution they think you are planning will be much worse than anything you could come up with yourself. By all means allow yourself the luxury of thinking up some nice new random acts of malevolence, but don't do anything about it just yet. Be tantric. Allow it all to fester for as long as you possibly can, then *BAM!* Hit them with it later, when they are least expecting it and when there will be no obvious link with the trigger incident.

If prevention has been impossible and you've blown, don't panic. I know of one senior manager who regularly throws her phone, laptop and other company equipment (never her own – remember that) around her office if someone does anything to displease her. This intimidates her boss as much as her staff, making them all too scared to fire her.

More usual, though, is the tendency to say or shout something inappropriate following an act of provocation. Whether this was a deliberate act by a particularly stupid or snide member of staff, or completely manufactured in your own head, does not matter a jot. When it happens, never apologise and don't try to be extra-nice to everyone afterwards. This idiot has pushed to you the very boundaries of your sanity. Send them out for a walk with instructions to think about what they can do to get their job back.

Losing it in front of witnesses is a rather more difficult situation from which to recover. Try not to do it. A client of mine once had a lapse of cool of Arctic-melting proportions in front of his boss, my boss and a bunch of other assorted bigwigs. As lapses go, it was a classic illustration of the three common types – throwing, swearing and sobbing – in one spectacular breakdown. He hurled a pile of documents at various people around the table, told my boss (the Chairman of a multinational company) to f*ck off, then burst into tears for the rest of the day. Fulsome apologies were made later by his boss, and the client was whisked away from his glitzy global marketing job to one where he spent the rest of his days tracking the movement of his company's lorries around the UK.

The point is that, if you have a momentary lapse of cool, try to avoid miring yourself in an irretrievable situation. You are going to blow, so prepare for it. What you need is a handy list of stock phrases that you repeat to yourself until they are hard-wired into your brain's speech centre. Innocuous phrases like "How did you get a job here?" or baffling ones like "I see that the spotted cuckoo sings early this year" – things that you can deliver at high volume or with chilling intensity, but still get away with. If out of context with the situation so much the better, since this confuses people and makes them shut up while their brain struggles to match what it's just heard with the situation it knows it's in. But remember: one phrase only, then walk away.

When that irritating Cardigan has slow-burned you to the point of explosion, these need to be the phrases you find yourself saying automatically. So much better than what your brain had in store for you. And you will look very grown up and mature. Well done you.

JUST REMEMBER

Always apologising after a blow-out is as dangerous as *never* apologising.

When it happens, absent yourself as soon as you can from the scene of the accident but return later to explain what it was that had tipped you over the edge and, if you really have to, offer a rare apology.

HOW TO WIN AT MEETINGS

"The object of war is not to die for your country but to make the other bastard die for his."
General Paton

Meetings are an exercise in survival, bringing to light all of the aggressive qualities of your team and allowing even the Cardigans to show off impressive passive-aggressive skills. How do you stop yourself being eaten alive? You can't take weapons in. Anyway, you don't just want to survive at meetings: you want to win – or, at least, not let them win.

Meetings, invariably, are used by your staff to enhance their position and undermine others, particularly those not present. This is an ideal opportunity to appear to be the champion of all your staff by defending the absent employee to the hilt even if he or she has made a complete hash of something, while at the same time slapping down the aggressor. It's ammunition in the bag should you need to use it against either of them later.

While meetings are an ideal opportunity to encourage those you are trying to nurture, they are also ideal opportunities to put down those who are more politically motivated (Category 2 staff, for example). Ruthlessly point out any faux pas or naïve statements made by those you feel are a threat. More importantly, don't let anyone other than you take the credit for a good idea. If a good idea is put forward ignore it, pass over it immediately, then reintroduce it yourself later. Take care not to let anyone else reintroduce it themselves.

Irritatingly, but with unerring regularity, someone at some point will say that something is "only common sense". In 1776 Thomas Paine, one of the founding fathers of the USA, wrote a book called Common Sense in which he presented the American colonists with a powerful argument for independence from British rule at a time when the question of independence was still undecided.

Unfortunately, when the phrase is used today, it tends not to mean that the "something" in question is the logical result of an argument. Far from it. In pointing out that something is "only common sense", the speaker is inferring that, if you disagree, you're an idiot. People frequently use this phrase to try and enforce an unsubstantiated prejudice or position. It is a confrontational stance that must be handled delicately and, whether you agree or disagree, it is important to make sure you maintain control of the situation.

The best way to do this is to insist on clarification as to why the issue in question must be treated as fact. The aggressor will then fall flat on his face as he will inevitably not have thought it through. Even if he has a point, by putting the onus on the aggressor to expound his argument fully, you have maintained your dominant position.

You may remember the importance of your own backside from an earlier chapter. It is likely that, at some point, usually during a staff meeting, your brain will decide to give your mouth a rest and decide to use your backside instead. While what you intend to say makes perfect sense to you in that moment, what you will hear is the emanation of something cringeworthy in the extreme; something worthy of David Brent in the TV documentary The Office. This is an involuntary response that you cannot control. If, in a staff meeting, you find a Brent-esque comment escaping, try and stop it. If it's too late, press on and act like nothing's happened.

JUST REMEMBER

Aim to talk and listen in sensible quantities. Note that the talking part does not necessarily need to involve original thought, and you can simply reiterate what someone else has said or thank them for their contribution. This still counts.

Even if you can't manage the ideal talking:listening ratio, make sure that it is you who introduces and summarises the meeting.

HELL IS OTHER PEOPLE: SURVIVING TEAM BUILDING EVENTS

"We Smell Fear"
Team motto for a US-based under-8s football team

If you work for a company that still thinks it's cool to torture people with organised fun, then this chapter is for you.

The economy of the developed world has been surely been seriously dented by the millions of sick days taken due to the natural desire to avoid team building exercises. You yourself may have done exactly that when faced by, say, two days of orienteering in the rain with a group of people that you would rather take out with an Uzi. There are many documented examples of mind-bogglingly pointless and pathetic team-building opportunities offered by companies who make a good living out of the misery of others (and your budget).

An example of a team-building day that nicely illustrates the twin criteria of pointless and pathetic was reported by an acquaintance who was once forced to spend a day in some far-flung corner of the countryside with his team. As a newly-appointed manager, he was required to place paper bags over the heads of his team then, equipped with a whistle, guide them into a sheeps' pen. He was 40 years old. Is this really the life you sign up for as a manager? How do you live with that? How can you possibly regain any dignity with your team?

The popularity of TV formats like *The X Factor* or *Dragons' Den* has had a knock-on effect in introducing a more judgemental aspect to team building. In the podgy, self-important hands of senior management, such ventures can produce unexpected results. Unexpectedly dangerous results. A company of my acquaintance organised a *Dragons' Den*-style team event in which staff were given a day to come up with ideas for a new business, all of which were subsequently ripped to shreds by the Dragons (the senior managers) who forgot that the whole thing was meant to be a bit of fun. Sure, the ultimate objective for the event was met in that the staff bonded alright, but in a negative, powerless fury against the management that still persists several years later.

So if the ugly subject of team building is raised, and if you have a choice in what the event will comprise, consider it carefully. The best that can happen is that you risk exposing yourself as incompetent in an activity that really doesn't matter, and it goes downhill from there.

Here is some guidance on what is OK and what is not OK when it comes to team building.

OK TEAM BUILDING IDEAS

A day at the races is OK, unless the new guy in your accounts department is about to be banged up for embezzlement he committed in his previous company to fund a long-term gambling habit. This actually happened. Checking someone's references, no matter how nice the person looks, is too important to be left to the HR department.

A night at the pub is also OK, unless you have a team of hopeless alcoholics. If you have a team of functioning alcoholics, however, then it is acceptable. This is common in many industry areas, and has been a badge of honour in the advertising business for the last 60 years.

If you're under pressure to introduce a competitive or educational element to the event, think about a night at a pub quiz. Charge the quiz entry fee and the first round of drinks to expenses, form a team of your best trivia heads, then sit back and have a well-earned rest.

If you work for the kind of company that would consider a pub quiz rather bargain basement, then hire the top floor of the Gherkin and a professional quizmaster, lay on a vat of champagne, and follow the instructions above.

TEAM BUILDING IDEAS THAT ARE *NOT* OK

Any event involving a swimming pool with underwater windows, unless you need to practice your buck-passing skills (see Evolution through Devolution).

Shooting, hunting, fishing, go-karting, orienteering, or any activity that involves being outside in unflattering shoes.

Any exercise that allows older men to be within grappling distance of younger women. There is an old ice-breaker ploy in which people are paired off and sheets of newspaper handed out, the challenge being for both people to stand on the newspaper in such a way that they are unable to touch each other.* In the wrong hands, this can descend into an abyss of groping and gurning that is not easily wiped from the memory.

JUST REMEMBER

People will always complain about whatever activity is chosen for team building. Don't worry about it.

The younger people will enjoy it more than the older ones. No-one has ever cracked the conundrum of how to ensure equal enjoyment for all. It is a fact of life.

---

* *The solution is to slide the newspaper underneath a solid barrier such as a door, with one half of the paper protruding from each side. Person A standing on one half of the paper will then be prevented from feeling up Victim B on the other side of the door.*

ENCOURAGING A RESIGNATION

"This is a case of the governor getting his way by the inflexion of his eyebrows."
Unnamed press source commenting on the encouragement of Bob Diamond (Barclays CEO) by Sir Mervyn King (Governor of the Bank of England) to resign after the 2012 Libor scandal

All experienced managers share a fantasy in which Lord Alan Sugar figures large. In the fantasy you are sitting across a very big desk from one of your team, pointing an assertive, if hairy, finger, and uttering the most satisfying half-dozen words in the English language: "You're a complete shambles. You're fired!"

Whatever kicks you get from indulging in this fantasy the truth is that, unless you are Lord Sugar, this will have to remain a pipe dream. Employment law and your own HR department have you in a pincer movement; try it and, unbelievably, you will be the one packing your lucky stapler and the photos of your kids into a cardboard box.

If all else has failed, and if you have put off the moment of firing for so long that the employee is now protected by law, then the best course open to you is to encourage a resignation. You could, of course, dispense with them based on their failure to achieve their performance targets but this risks all sorts of unpleasantness that you may not feel like dealing with. Far better to get them to fall on their sword than be the one to drive it though them.

The main confounding factor in cases such as this is one of perception: the individual will firmly believe that they are not managed properly (obviously a complete calumny) while you will know beyond all doubt that they are a malingering con artist and a hopeless case. In the middle is a potentially confused area of perception that makes you vulnerable to accusations of poor management should any independent enquiry bother to ask any awkward questions (you know what they are). Your efforts should be directed at claiming the area of vulnerability for yourself: to have clearly established their hopelessness beyond all doubt. But how?

The answer to the "I'm not managed properly" complaint is micromanagement. It takes a lot of work and attention to set someone up for failure. Yet ironically it will be the very thing that catalyses their departure. You will, of course, have already set them goals that they have failed to meet, and documented that in emails or notes of discussions with them. You may also, following the example of Sir Mervyn King, have inflected your eyebrows at them until your face ached. Some will be clever enough to read the writing on the wall and seek their fortune elsewhere. But others, whether unable to read the signs or cynical enough to ignore them, will remain comfortably in their uselessness until you do something to tip the balance.

If, despite having given the underperforming employee every chance of turning things around, they (and you) are still living in an unhappy marriage, then it is time to propel them gently towards divorce. Top of your mind should be the issue of unfair dismissal: even if they resign, you are not protected from a claim. So make sure that you do nothing to change the conditions of their job unacceptably or be seen to coerce them into leaving. Get advice from a good employment lawyer. Then be as honest as you can under the circumstances and edge the hopeless case ever closer to freedom.

Once you have someone in the departure lounge, the golden rule of pushing them towards the exit door is never to put anything vaguely encouraging or praiseworthy in writing. They will use it against you later. Continue to give them tasks even though you know they will continue to fail. This sounds harsh but, if they are not up to the job that they are being paid to do, then failure is the only realistic outcome. Meet with them regularly for a "state of the union" discussion and remind them of it by memo or email – you may need the evidence later. Phrase things along the lines of "I've tried everything I can to design a job for you that you will find fulfilling/can be competent at, but nothing has worked; now I need to hear from you how you plan to move forward". Then crush their plan on the basis of superficiality, unworkability or misalignment with business needs. Document that, too. Call your recruitment consultants and tell them that X is not a good fit with your team, but would be spectacular elsewhere.

Do everything in your power to make it obvious to the hopeless case that they are just not up to the job, while briefing motivated other parties, like recruitment consultants or colleagues with lower standards, to make a buck out of them elsewhere. A simple push-pull strategy. Or, if you want a quick win and are happy to live with some damage to your reputation as a manager, just get HR involved (see next section).

This sounds harsh, but you can't afford to forget the effect that a hopeless case, often earning a high salary, has on the rest of your team. How demotivating for a lower-paid, but productive, team member to see a highly-paid hopeless case doing nothing. This is one of your responsibilities as a manager: to ensure fairness and equity. It's a burden, one that is far less satisfying than the Lord Sugar fantasy, but one from which the confident manager will sneakily derive his own enjoyment.

BASIC MANAGEMENT ALGORITHM

All staff challenges can be approached using a simple management algorithm. The first question you should ask yourself is this: "Is this person useful to me?"

If the answer is *yes*, you have three further options:

1. Is this person **compliant**? If they are happy to go along with your plans, pay them enough to stay and behave themselves.

2. Is this person **challenging**? If this person is a pain in the neck, impose your authority using some of the tips in this book and bring them down a rung or two.

3. Is this person **a threat**? If so, patronise them with praise and load on the work. Take the credit for being far-sighted enough to spot and nurture their potential.

If the answer is *no*, you have two simple options:

1. Is this person **a liability**? If someone is dangerous to you and your team, you don't have time to engineer a resignation. Instead, engineer their transfer to someone else's team at the earliest possible opportunity.

2. Is this person **mostly harmless**? If so, re-emphasise their objectives and continue to try and get them to do their job while you wait for them to resign.

JUST REMEMBER

It is not fair to the rest of the team to tolerate someone who is just not up to the job for whatever reason. Terminating someone's employment is often something that is done *for* the rest of your hardworking team, not *against* the individual who is being fired.

Money spent on a good employment solicitor is never wasted.

YOU CANNOT TRUST HR

"HR are a bit like estate agents – they pretend to be on both sides but really they are on the side that's paying them".
Unnamed source quoted in *The Guardian* newspaper

First of all, a message to all trustworthy and competent HR people reading this section. You are a small but vital minority doing an important but often thankless job. To managers who have to work with HR departments, however, beware. Many HR professionals are anything but.

It all went off piste some years ago when, in a pathetic bid to big-up an essentially bureaucratic role, someone decided to change the nomenclature from "Personnel" to "Human Resources". Since HR is staffed by the chronically hard of thinking no-one thought to point out that this new terminology, far from emphasising the "human" aspect of the role, actually dehumanises it. Staff are regarded as a resource in the same way as printer cartridges or the office water supply and HR do not understand why they cannot be managed as such. Surely any resource can be turned on and off, upscaled or downscaled, or reallocated to an area of greater need – what could be more straightforward? Failure to achieve this instantly and without complaint from your staff is regarded as poor management.

But, you may be asking yourself, why should I worry about what HR thinks? It is there to support me as a manager and help me in the occasional battle with my team.

Wrong.

HR is the CEO's whore. It has a constant conflict of interest. Never forget that HR's boss is whoever owns or runs the company. Unless there is someone in the HR department with some vestige of conscience or judgement, they will drop you in it without a second thought. To them you are just another employee. In a situation where there is an allegation, however groundless, against you by a member of staff, the involvement of HR will lead at best to permanent damage to your reputation in the eyes of your management and at worst to a dual resignation: yours and that of the employee who caused the trouble.

The reason that most HR employees cannot be trusted is twofold. First, they answer to the big boss and are used as an implement to impose his or her will on the team. Second, they do not themselves understand the basic rules of management, some of which require a light touch to get the best result. HR employees approach all staffing issues with their Big Book of HR in one hand and a sledgehammer in the other. This, on top of a general lack of good judgement, is guaranteed to have spectacular effects if you are watching from a distance. If, however, you are involved at the core of the issue, watch out for your nuts.

Here are some examples, all true, of circumstances where HR involvement has truly screwed things up:

Contacting a candidate's old employer for a reference before the candidate had resigned. *Result*: candidate was fired before he could resign, and demanded a golden hello as compensation. *Cost to company*: Thousands of pounds.

Mishandling the amicable departure of a senior member of staff. *Result*: the departing employee sued the company for constructive dismissal. *Cost to company*: tens of thousands of pounds.

Suspecting an employee of committing a criminal act, but not reporting it to the police. *Result*: employee threatened the company with a claim for unfair dismissal. *Cost to company*: thousands of pounds.

Overpaying an employee for two years, only finding out their mistake when the employee was promoted. Recouping the overpayment by slashing the newly-promoted employee's salary. *Result*: employee, demotivated by a reduced salary for more hours and greater responsibility, found a job elsewhere. *Cost to company*: one good man plus unrecovered overpaid salary.

Mishandling the redundancy of an employee. *Result*: situation rescued by senior manager with better judgement.

Cost to company: a greatly enhanced redundancy package for the unfortunate reduntantee.

Concealing information from company director A on the orders of company director B. *Result*: departure of director A from company and threat of serious legal action. *Cost to company*: hundreds of thousands of pounds.

Conducting a risk assessment for a pregnant worker in which she was instructed not to work past 5.30pm. However, because the HR representative was so busy and important, he could not conduct the assessment before 7.30pm. *Result*: a vastly improved understanding of irony on the part of the mother-to-be. *Cost to company*: Minimal, to be fair.

Whatever chaos HR causes, it is unfortunately your responsibility as a manager to try and maintain some semblance of control and to do what you can to rescue a bad situation. This is not always easy. Take the example, perfectly true, of the occasion when HR convinced a troublesome and poorly performing employee to stay with the company after his manager had successfully engineered his resignation. To this day, the employee is still drawing a salary from the company, having celebrated his decision to stay by interspersing the odd grudging appearance at the office with long periods of sickness (stress, naturally). His performance, poor at best, hit a new low and stayed there. His bitching skills, on the other hand, honed themselves to perfection. But, of course, by now he was unsackable. The manager, horribly undermined, never recovered her credibility and eventually left the company after giving HR the benefit of a viciously informative exit interview.

In this situation it is difficult to know what more the manager could have done to impose her authority, but a complaint about HR to her own manager might have helped her claw back some credibility by showing that she was not afraid to make a major stink when needed.

The HR department hides its workings behind the need for confidentiality. Indeed, this adherence to confidentiality masks all kinds of incompetence and can be incredibly divisive when used heavy-handedly in conjunction with the Big Book of HR. Manager can be turned against manager, employee against employee, manager against team and vice versa. It is worth taking the time to find out exactly what you as a manager could and should be told about your team, and then ensuring that you are kept informed. For example, if one of your team is off sick, HR should give you sufficient information so that you can plan how to deliver the team's work over the long term. While you don't need to know about the person's illness in all its gory detail, you need some indication of whether they are likely to be off for a week, a month or a year.

A discussion with your HR department on what you are entitled to know, followed by a discussion with your boss if you don't get a co-operative response, should be towards the top of your list of things to do. Once the general principles are established, make sure that HR sticks to the deal. If you subsequently find out about something they should have told you, point it out to them. The right to confidentiality is there to protect the employee, not the HR department.

So how to use HR for good? No-one really knows. When things blow up in your face, you can make it clear that it is HR who is responsible for providing advice on what action to take. You can point out that they are the experts, they understand employment law and you wouldn't dream of telling them how to do their job. Distance yourself from the process as much as you can then, when it all goes nuclear, you can blame it on them.

This approach works well for people you want to lose from your team.

If, however, there is an issue with someone you rate, someone who is useful to you, then your first step should always be to see if you can resolve things directly with them either via a shouting match in a soundproofed meeting room or a quiet drink in the pub. Forget your principles. Beg for forgiveness. Abase yourself if you have to. However much you prostitute yourself it cannot be worse than calling in the professionals.

Just Remember

In the eyes of HR you are just another employee. They act for whoever owns or runs the company, not for you.

If you can resolve team issues without the need for HR, great. If not then make it clear that, as the professionals, it is their responsibility to provide advice on the best course of action but that, as the manager, the final call is yours.

RECRUITMENT: SATAN'S BINGO

"Only in Britain could it be thought a defect to be 'too clever by half.' The probability is that too many people are too stupid by three-quarters."
John Major

Don't let anyone tell you that any recruitment process is strategic. It's about as strategic as a game of bingo, but with people involved. This makes it even more unpredictable and less likely that you'll win.

In a misguided stint in the headhunting business I interviewed hundreds of candidates and can vouch for the idiocy of normally sensible people in a job-hunting situation. The graduate who wanted to "excellerate" her career who, when her mistake was pointed out, claimed that the word was not in the dictionary so how could she check it? The chancers who tell you they don't want the job but "how about a drink?" These people gradually chip away at your faith in the working public and, more worryingly, erode your ability to regard human beings as individuals. You will struggle to maintain your ability to distinguish between different people, not to mention your humanity, as you writhe impotently in the purgatory that is Satan's bingo.

People with whom you struggle to maintain a conversation are out. Candidates who have been wrongly briefed by the recruitment consultant and who are expecting a line-management position when there isn't one are out. People who are clearly a bad fit with your team are out. In these cases, end the interview early but civilly. There is no point in wasting the time of either party when things are so obviously not going to work.

If you find yourself subsumed by a heap of nauseating flattery from a candidate, steer well clear. Chances are that you are sitting across the desk from a Politician. If you are naïve enough to give them the job it's a racing certainty that, the minute their probationary period is over, they will transfer their attention to your boss or anyone else more useful to them. You will simply cease to exist in their world. You will be a ghost. Your attempts at management will have the impact of a fart in a wind tunnel. In ignoring you and flattering your bosses, they become completely unmanageable and make you look like a failure. Don't fall for it.

It is impossible to tell from a CV whether a candidate is right for the job. It is equally impossible to tell even after several rounds of interviews. Most companies have the odd employee of several years' standing where the jury is still out. In other words, it is simply not possible to find out whether someone has been a good hire until they prove that they can do the job *in situ*.

When someone does not work out, your boss will make you feel as if you have somehow failed, and that your recruitment skills leave a lot to be desired. This is, of course, nonsense and should not be allowed to put even the dinkiest of dinks in your self-esteem. Protect yourself by involving your boss in the recruitment process. Even though he or she will do their best not to give a firm opinion on the candidate you want (in case they fail), make sure you give them the right of veto. Then, when a candidate fails, your boss will at least have to shoulder some of the responsibility. After all, they should be able to spot a hopeless case and protect you from it – that is their role as your manager.

If someone works out, however, accept the stroke of luck and take the credit.

While it is tempting to devolve at least part of the recruitment process to someone who doesn't duck quickly enough, this can be a timewaster if not properly managed. I recently heard of a company that needed a part-time office assistant; someone to work a few hours a day, possibly in between school runs, to order FedExes, queue at the post office, get sandwiches for meetings, keep an eye on the toilet roll supply…the little things that keep an office running smoothly. The task was devolved to a manager to select a shortlist of likely candidates for interview. Of 125 replies, he picked five, three of whom had university degrees, one of which was from Oxford University. He had ranked each of the applications according to the following criteria:

1. *Was a covering letter supplied?*
OK, so far, so sensible.
2. *Was the CV well laid out?*
Fair enough — a good eye for presentation is a plus.
3. *Did the candidate have relevant qualifications?*

In *what* exactly? Checking teabag supplies? Sandwich fetching? An MBA?

All of the people who would have been happy to earn money doing a basic office administration job had been binned, while those with aspirations to "get on" — ie. those who already felt they were too good for the job — had been selected. If this happens to you then tell the manager in question that he is in possession of the wrong end of the stick and publicly redo the selection process yourself. While it is admittedly more work for you it will emphasise your dominance, win the loyalty of the successful candidate (to whom you will obviously tell the story at some point), and make you look extremely decisive and managerial.

JUST REMEMBER

No-one ever knows how a candidate is going to work out. If they are a disaster, there is in all likelihood nothing more you could have done at interview so don't allow yourself to be criticised for it.

Don't waste your time interviewing people you know are not suitable just because you are desperate to fill the position or because you think you should be more "creative" in your approach to finding candidates. These are precious hours of your life that you will never get back.

THESE PEOPLE ARE NOT YOUR FAMILY

"An ounce of blood is worth more than a pound of friendship."
Spanish proverb

If you are ever offered a management position in a family company, and if that family is not your own, then take just one word of advice. Don't. In case that didn't convince you, here are some more words: Run. Away.

If you have been cleverly suckered into joining someone else's family company, then your primary objective has to be to get out of there while you are still ahead.

The trouble with family companies is that, no matter how good you are or how much you contribute to the success of that company, one of the family will eventually cock up. When that happens – and it will – the family will close ranks. This signals the beginning of a parting of the ways. As the Outsider, your best-case scenario is that the direction in which you thought the company was going will change in a way that you don't like. The worst-case scenario is that you carry the can for the initial screw-up and all future mistakes made as a direct or indirect result of the imbecilic family member who caused the problem in the first place. This is when you start to realise that, whatever you have done for the company in the past, whatever sacrifices you've made, however many birthdays and school plays you've missed to deal with business matters, you suddenly don't count.

As an old friend's father said on the day of her divorce, "Every village has an idiot. Why did you have to go and marry it?" It's the same with a family-run business. Lots of families have one. But why did you have to go and work for it?

The key to getting out alive is to understand the facts that underpin and govern the dynamics of the company. The typical family company is founded on "the four – isms". They are:

Nepotism

Idiot family members will be given precedence. They just will. Live with it or get the hell out.

Protectionism

A family will always shore up their resident idiot by doing their work for them, letting them off when they have failed at something and, most importantly, supporting them and their imbecilic ventures with money that you have earned. You will see profit poured without limit into the gullet of a wastrel, profit for which you have suffered daily at the hands of your staff. And all this because they share some genetic code with the others (or, worse, are sleeping with someone who shares those genes).

Egotism

This leads to bad decision-making, a total inability to communicate with Outsiders, and an irrepressible itch to interfere with the smooth workings of the team that you run. This is dangerous. These people are usually bullies. The last thing you want is to have someone else bullying your team.

Priapism

The head of the family has the biggest dick and it is constantly pointing UP. Regardless of whether he (or she) does or not, this is what the entire family will believe. However many times, and by whatever means, you try to prove them wrong, you will not be able to do it. The more you wave it about, the more they will ignore it and the more you will feel like the pathetic raincoat-clad flasher in the park that you are. Save it for someone who will appreciate it and start looking for another job now.

When things start going wrong, and you realise that you are now perceived as nothing more than a minor irritant by the train-wreck of DNA that passes for your employers or partners, it is time to plan your exit. Do not let it get to the point where you become a major irritant by speaking your mind. You must be a "good leaver", ideally leaving with the home phone numbers of a few good staff and any business contacts that can help you in your next job.

JUST REMEMBER

Don't join a family company unless you really, really need the money.

Think twice before challenging any of the family members and, if you do, spend time planning out very carefully how you are going to approach it.

PART II

The Facts of Life

JASON LYE

GROWING UP IS HARD TO DO

"You grow up the day you have the first real laugh at yourself."
Ethel Barrymore

Do you ever sit at your desk wondering why you feel so mentally beaten up? Is this happening with increasing regularity, and within half an hour of arriving at work? Look up and you see your manager. Look around and you see your colleagues. Look under your feet and you see the team that you are supposed to be managing. Are you going round in circles? Then you are the hub of what, in management terms, can be thought of as the workplace cartwheel of doom.

Together, your managers and your team are forcing you to be someone you sometimes don't recognise, to behave in a way that is often anathema to the real you, and to live in a way that you don't really like all that much.

Now that you've reached the ranks of management (or even if you haven't), it's time to take some responsibility for yourself, grow a thicker skin and stop these people trying to make you live the wrong life. Are you ready to put your foot down and refuse to live the life that they want you to live? Are you ready to find your own way of getting on in your career? Then read on.

This section looks at the facts of life you need to know in order to grow in your role, to develop as a useful team member and manager, and to avoid prison for physical assault on your colleagues.

When you first heard of the facts of life as a child, your reaction was probably to think "Are you insane? My parents would never do that." But as you grow up, you find yourself doing exactly the same stuff.

The same is true in your work life. At first sight, the office facts of life are ghastly and unfathomable. But every day of your working existence is another step towards understanding and accepting these strange things that we all do. As you arrive at the next level of management you'll start to find them sustaining, sometimes even pleasurable.

Perhaps the most important fact of life, and one that goes largely unappreciated by those yet to scale the vomit-inducing heights of management, is this. Everyone has a boss. You have one. They have one. Even the chairman has one – the shareholders. And anyone with management responsibility, at whatever level, is bossed around – by the staff. Remember that the power struggle cuts both ways.

Think of a boss as someone (or something) who can intimidate, control and occasionally nurture you, something that can threaten you, praise you, withdraw privileges or reward you. See? You have to answer to your team as much as to your manager. But don't think that you can rely on your own management to be at your side when scrapping it out with your team. The truth is that they prefer to have you in front.

Whoever or whatever your boss is, you need to remember two important facts:

1. They don't always act in your interest. Mainly, they act in their own interest.

2. Like you, your boss is usually making it up as he or she goes along.

You are left with no choice but to start thinking for yourself, to protect yourself from both your manager and your team. You'll find yourself musing on the rights and wrongs of situations, gradually driving yourself to the brink of insanity as you work out your own opinions on the minutiae of management.

Like you, your manager will make mistakes. Some will be forgivable: simple acts of thoughtlessness or forgetfulness that are nothing personal. On the other hand, some will be unforgivable. In the latter category will inevitably be things that they have really thought about – really stupid things – and decided to implement. At the same time, your workmates and the lucky people who report to you will torture you in other ways. Sometimes they mean it.

In any case, the façade of a well-adjusted adult is necessary if you are to preserve your dignity and advance your career under the combined onslaught of your managers and staff. If you're not particularly well-adjusted, then you will just have to rein in any particularly unpleasant natural tendencies during the working day. But, whatever the situation, be true to yourself. And if being true to yourself involves minor acts of revenge, there's nothing wrong with that.

JUST REMEMBER

You don't have to play along with anything stupid. You're a grown up now. Use your judgement.

Do your job to the best of your ability with a good grace, and go home at night to your real life. If your job *is* your main purpose in life and you enjoy it despite the people problems, read on. This may help you get things in perspective.

YOU CAN RUN AWAY FROM DIFFICULT QUESTIONS

"The definition of style is when they are running you out of town and you make it look as if you're leading a parade."
William Battie

"You look like a million dollars – is that how much it cost?" was Clive Anderson's opening question in an interview with Cher. Brutal, you may think, but it's nothing compared to some of the interrogation you will face in your role as a manager.

As the leader of a team, you will be thrown to the wolves by your management on regular occasions. Your future rests on your ability to implement your boss's will; to manipulate your team into obedience and, in the process, to answer some difficult questions. Questions to which you yourself might not know the answer, either because you weren't paying attention or because you have not been let in on the whole picture by your own managers.

The problem is that the questions you'll be asked really should be possible to answer. They will not be intrinsically impossible questions like "Do snails dream?" or "Is it possible to shoot a wasp?" They won't even be questions that sap you of your intellectual power, such as "Late 20th century literature provided us with no heroic protagonists. Discuss." Or that involve some diabolical choice, such as "Would you rather have sex with Boris Johnson and no-one know, or not have sex with him and have everyone think you did?"

On the contrary, they will be questions that you should be able to deal with and, moreover, that you are probably morally obliged to answer in full.

Let's say someone asks you to explain why, despite your team beating their targets by a mile, they are getting only a minimal bonus. You know it's because the company overall has had a terrible year due to mismanagement by your own bosses, but have been sworn to secrecy about the scale of the devastation they have wreaked. Or at least, that's what you think you know: you had zoned out at the relevant management meeting after hearing the words "significant", "challenge" and "up shit creek" repeated once too often.

Don't despair. There are a number of ways in which you can deal with this kind of question without revealing your own ignorance. Here are five of them.

1. **Attack the question**. "Minimal? In the current economic environment, I wouldn't call a 0.1% bonus minimal. How do you define minimal?"

2. **Throw doubt on the questioner**. "I'm surprised to hear this question from you, Darren, because you have always done very well out of the company."

3. **Compliment the questioner, then ask a completely different question**. "That's a very good question and I'm glad you brought it up. Of course, what you're really asking is how did I manage to get agreement for your bonuses given the challenges the company has faced this year."

4. **Debunk the question**. Sometimes the questioner will preface the question with a loaded statement such as "Lots of people are upset about your decision to award derisory bonuses this year." This leaves you no option but to say "Name six."

5. **Confuse everyone with a long, pointless answer until they give up and go away**. In other words, turn an ambush into a war of attrition by styling it out. Just make sure you have enough time and sugary snacks to outlast your opponents and win.

Ultimately, your aim is to get people to understand that the only question ever worth asking you is "Your Grace (or whatever you make them call you). Why don't you just tell me what the answer is to my next question?"

JUST REMEMBER

People have a right to ask whatever questions they want, but they don't necessarily have the right to an answer.

When asked a question that you can't answer for whatever reason, keep calm and blag it off with conviction.

YOU CAN'T AVOID THE OCCASIONAL HUMILIATION, SO BRACE YOURSELF

"A consultant told us what kind of animal each of us was. The boss turned out to be a lion (surprise!). I was a monkey. My colleagues were told that they weren't allowed to tell me to tidy my workspace because it would stifle my natural simian creativity."
Anonymous

Unless you've been super-lucky, you will have had to endure several management training or bonding events over the course of your career as your managers try to potty train you in your role. Now that you have scaled the heady heights of management, it becomes your job to inflict this nonsense on the next generation. No training for managers is worth its salt unless it contains a sprinkling of cold fear followed up by a massive bucketful of unforgettable humiliation.

Not so long ago, a large communications company hired external consultants to take up temporary residence in their offices, make a fuss of the managers and make it look as though these lucky people were receiving some training and motivation.

The consultants duly showed up, infiltrating the middle layer of management like a swarm of demented ants. All managers were interviewed individually and given pathetically facile exercises to do. For example, in intimate one-to-one sessions with a consultant, each manager was required to draw a picture of how they viewed their team and their role as leader. The drawing served as the basis for a private chat about the problems and frustrations the manager was facing, and how some of these issues might be resolved.

An old colleague of mine who was, at the time, a department head at the company, drew an honest and detailed picture of how she perceived her situation. She drew herself trapped in a room, bars on the windows, looking out to an open-plan office. In the office she depicted half her staff as fist-fighting yobs and the other half slumped at their desks, possibly asleep.

She thought it an honest portrait of her situation, and a nice illustration of her feelings of hopelessness and despair in the face of her underlings – which, as a fellow manager, you will no doubt recognise. The management consultants took away the drawings produced by each manager, no doubt to pin on the fridge at their nest. My friend thought no more about it, other than experiencing a welcome feeling of relief and appreciation at having had the opportunity to share her frustrations with a friendly ear.

Some months later, an invitation arrived to a management workshop, to be held at a swanky country house hotel. The same consultants were there, having put together a programme of even more time-wasting and patronising exercises. Imagine my friend's surprise when they whipped out the managers' drawings, and invited each manager on to a platform at the front of the room to present and explain their drawing to everyone else. "Everyone else" included the Chairman and the rest of the board.

One of my friend's colleagues had depicted himself as a juggler, explaining with a straight face that he was so busy that he felt like a circus juggler, skilfully keeping his balls in the air, so to speak, with the explanation that his role was to ensure that his high-flying team stayed airborne and co-ordinated.

Another had drawn a picture of a racing car speeding across a finish line, and gave some bollocks explanation about how he sees himself as the driver of a high-performance vehicle that always likes to win.

Getting up to present her Munch-like portrait of real life, as my friend now says, "That's when I knew I was fucked."

Of course, it's not just training that causes peak humiliation opportunities for management. Companies are finding ever-more inventive and misguided ways of stuffing up the relationship between management and staff. See if you can better these examples – and, if you do, let me know.

Another friend once worked for the UK offshoot of a large and very well-known US company which prides itself on its high ethical standards and family values. One day, management decided to rationalise all email addresses, reducing them to the first initial, the first five letters of the surname, and a number @company.com. Let's say my friend's name was Michael Stevenson. He showed up as msteve1@company.com. His only ally at work, and the only other truly efficient person in the department, had the misfortune to have been christened Thomas Watson.

Sadly, Thomas' parents had failed to predict the new naming convention of his company. After the email "improvements" Thomas showed up on the email directory and in all of his clients' inboxes as twatso1@company.com.

He asked the company to change his email name, explaining repeatedly and with increasing creativity the meaning of the word "twats" to the US-based IT bosses. After some weeks of increasingly desperate negotiation, the IT department made a concession. They were prepared to change his email name to twatso2@company.com. Thus demoting Thomas to a second-rate twat. After many more months of fruitless begging, and with the now permanent nickname of Twatso, Thomas left for a company with a more sensible email naming policy.

Here's another example. Just last year, new levels of incompetence at a cash-strapped academic institution somewhere in the UK prompted the departure of a head of department. Turning the volume dial up to 11 while simultaneously pressing the nuclear button, the said head of department left with a voluble and comprehensive dissection of the shortcomings of senior management. Shortly afterwards, the staff were called to a meeting where they were told that the head of department would not be replaced, and that some of the money saved on not filling his role would be redistributed among the staff as a bonus.

They were then forced to play *Bruce Forsyth's Play Your Cards Right* as their managers made them guess the amount of their bonus.

Embarrassed mutterings of "higher" and "lower" were coerced from the lucky bonus recipients – at least, from those of them old enough to remember the show. Some still get upsetting flashbacks of shame and embarrassment at the memory. And so the management instilled feelings of such deep self-loathing within their staff that most cannot bear to be reminded of it and are looking for a saner existence elsewhere.

Using a similar expert management approach, a particularly objectionable CEO of my acquaintance organised a big "I am" series of meetings, ostensibly to update everyone on the company's progress but actually to satisfy his own self-important needs. During the meetings, he ranked each of the company's teams on a five-point "pints of beer" scale. So what he considered to be the best performer was awarded five pints of beer, and the worst one pint.

Not only were the staff appalled at being judged in this manner (there was vehement disagreement with his scoring) but they couldn't believe that he still thought beer analogies were cool. The headhunters' phones have been ringing off the hook ever since.

The moral of all this is twofold. First, never underestimate the decency of normal individuals. Not everyone is as venal as the newspapers and shows like The Apprentice would have you believe. And second, don't, whatever you do, use crass or outmoded analogies to get your point across. If you're going to resort to analogies, find one from the current century, or at least something that didn't happen before half your team were born.

If the worst happens and you are humiliated either as an individual or as one of a group, do whatever you need to do to save face. Make light of it, joke about it, adopt a mature attitude and reduce its significance. Rise above it all, but never forget. One day you'll get the chance for revenge. Take it.

If you yourself are under pressure to humiliate an individual or a group of people, either directly or as the henchman of someone more senior, you're facing one of the greatest ethical decisions of your career. Do you play along or not? Only you can decide. But whatever you decide, remember that it's something you'll have to live with for the rest of your life.

JUST REMEMBER

Most people are decent, many are shy, and everyone finds contrived situations cringeworthy and embarrassing. Bear this in mind when training and evaluating your troops. You can't change people's personalities, so don't force them into humiliating situations.

Think twice before turning the spotlight on individuals, departments or companies. If you want them to know what you think of them, at least give them a heads-up before telling them in front of everyone else.

SOMETIMES YOU ARE FORCED TO REPORT TO A NUTTER

"Every murderer is probably somebody's old friend."
Agatha Christie

Many kinds of nutter make it to the upper echelons of management. Some have been moved there out of harm's way, leaving other, more competent people to keep the wheels on the cart. Others, particularly those who have set up their own companies, may have an innate personal quirkiness which perhaps has been part of their success. When benign, both of these are generally harmless and easily managed: the incompetent boss by telling him what he needs to know and the quirky entrepreneur by flattery and wit.

Much more difficult to cope with is the malignant nutter, of which there are three main types: the spoilt brat, the irritating bore, and the scary one. So what can you do when one of the most influential people in the company is a malignant nutter and it's your job to report to it?

Let's start by trying to understand these silly people just a little bit better.

Category 1. The spoilt brat

This is often someone who started out perfectly normal, but who has been spoiled by indulgent management. More often than not, this person has been protected along the way: perhaps they are someone who has been a protégé of the big boss, or perhaps they have been appointed by a family member. Or maybe they are a family member, from the idiot branch.

As a result of all the mollycoddling, the psyche of this person becomes irreversibly deformed. They believe that they are good at their job because their protector has over-encouraged them. They are indulged in their brattishness by the parental behaviour of their protectors. In short, they are like spoilt children.

These people are volcanos waiting to blow. And, when they do, they cover those around them with hot, molten, smelly, moody and painful lava. These are the people who can't be reasoned with, who don't think logically (or at all), and who cause good staff to resign.

They are dangerous. Brave management will get rid of them, or at least contain them in an area where they can do little harm. However, distressingly few senior managers are brave. More often than not, these brats will end up in positions of power, protected rather than dealt with, and eventually somehow your problem.

Sometimes the spoilt brat is more exasperating than dangerous. Here's a good example of irritating spoilt brat behaviour. I once travelled to Sweden with the head of client services of the company I worked for. On the plane he complained continually about everything, loudly and annoyingly like a demonic six-year-old. Why did the crew bring the food first? They should bring the drinks first. Where was his drink? Why did his seat not recline further? Why was I – or anyone – in the seat next to him? How could he be expected to work under these conditions? Mortally embarrassed, I slunk as low as possible in my seat and waited for the flight to be over.

The following day we returned to the UK on different flights. As my plane took off, the stranger in the seat next to me turned to me and said "I recognise you from the flight last night." I nodded nervously.

Then, with stunning perspicacity, he said, "Who was that arsehole you were with?"

A lasting friendship was struck up there and then.

Category 2. The irritating bore

Not always obviously malignant, the irritating bore has a much more insidious effect on the people around him. This effect will be to drive you steadily and irreversibly insane over a long period of time.

One of the characteristics of the irritating bore is an excellent memory for facts and trivia, but an intellectual feebleness that makes him unable to develop anything interesting out of it.

This kind of nutter has no insight into the effect of the grinding tedium he inspires in those around him. He will have amusing sayings that he will trot out on a regular basis. For example he may repeat ad infinitum some old saying, like "There's nothing worse than setting the bar low, then missing", and follow it up with that irritating avuncular chuckle that you have come to despise so greatly. Or he will launch into an anecdote from 20 years ago that you and everyone else have heard a gadzillion times. Or he may start a conversation from a position of such extreme bias and stupidity that you have no option but to place yourself at the other end of the scale. You then find yourself defending a position that you don't yourself believe in, but which the nutter has forced you into simply through his unthinking ignorance.

This is the way he manages people: by hints, random anecdotes and chronic erosion of spirit.

You will find it increasingly difficult not to join in sarcastically with his well-trodden recitations while miming slitting your wrists. Or, as an attractive alternative, you could give serious consideration to slinking off and eating your own spleen in quiet and unobtrusive despair.

Category 3. The scary one

When the scary one makes it to the top, everyone's in trouble. You most of all if you have to work with it (whether it's a man or a woman is irrelevant). These people can turn a minor disagreement into a longstanding personal vendetta. Masters in the art of choosing to take things personally, they keep everyone walking on eggshells, administering the odd swift kick to keep their team off-balance, and occasionally reducing the weaker, or nicer, members of their teams to tears.

You can't stand up to them in case of a flare-up. But constantly giving in to their crazy demands risks being viewed with derision by all those around you – and, perhaps, even by the nutter himself who will not even do you the basic courtesy of appreciating your arse-licking tact.

All scary nutters share a common way of thinking based on syllogism. In its earliest form, Aristotle defined a syllogistic argument thus:

All men are mortal
Socrates is a man
Therefore Socrates is mortal

Unfortunately, the scary nutter tends generally not to be too hot on the basics of philosophy or on grasping any line of thinking longer than five words. To them a syllogism goes something like this:

All dogs have four legs
My cat has four legs
Therefore my cat is a dog

Or, more commonly and much more unfortunately for you:

I must shout at someone
You are someone
Therefore I must shout at you

Sometimes the scary one is a pathological controller, with an uncontrollable urge to play god with people and situations.

Sometimes they are frighteningly unpredictable. Being assigned to work for one of these is a little like being found a play date by your parents. But your play buddy turns out to be fascinated by matches and is forever setting things on fire. Never let them chain you to an arsonist. I myself used to work with someone like this, who kept his staff in a permanent state of alert thanks to his constant unpredictability of mood. His long-suffering team, paranoid to the last man and woman, dared not even use words to let each other know how much trouble they were in on any given day. Instead they relied on highlighter pens, displayed on their desks in a sophisticated system of colour combinations for different threat levels, to alert their team-mates to the prevailing state of insanity raging inside the head of their boss. While it could be argued that this impressive creativity, organisation and team co-operation was inspired by the boss, it's really not something you want to aim for.

Sometimes the nutter is not so much scary as sinister. They are a shiver waiting for a spine to run up. There's nothing you can quite put your finger on, apart from overwhelming apprehension, a non-specific fear that something bad is going to happen, and a reluctance to be alone with them in the same room with the door shut. In this case, before you join in the general bitchery, you need to make sure that the person is properly malignant, not just misunderstood.

You'll find that nutters of whatever variety will have differing levels of insight into their behaviour. Some have occasional flashes of self awareness, and try and compensate for their latest act of loonery by doing something nice that nobody wants. The rest are oblivious to their behaviour and blame the effects of it on the simple-mindedness of their staff.

But what the malignant nutter doesn't realise is that they have a valuable role in the company. That role is as a focus for everyone's hatred. If your team is busy hating one person, then they have less time to spend on infighting or torturing you as their manager.

This is how you learn to live with the nutter. Use it to deflect criticism from you, and as a way to bond with your team. Never insult the nutter explicitly in front of anyone else, but concentrate on developing these important skills.

1. The art of the wry smile.

Listen impassively, giving the occasional understanding smile but without passing comment. To agree with anything the nutter says is dangerous, particularly if it follows a stream of invective about how hopeless everyone is, how slowly the work is progressing, and how poorly the department is performing.

The moment you agree with them is the moment you kill your own relationship with your colleagues. Because the nutter will eventually end up implying to them them that all of that invective came from you.

2. Flattery with or without a hint of sarcasm.

You can try to stem the flow of invective by flattering the nutter. Turning the topic of conversation around to the charm and positive characteristics of the nutter knocks them off the topic of negativity towards the staff. Everyone likes to be praised.

Whatever degree of subtle sarcasm you inject into the conversation is up to you. Generally the more bonkers the nutter, the more fun you can have.

3. Perhaps the best way to deal with a nutter – and the way that is most likely to keep you and your team sane – is this. **Make light of the nutter's foibles in a way that totally undermines them and/or find a suitable nickname that makes them look stupid**.

For example, the manager who thought up the *Play Your Cards Right* gambit might have been christened "Brucie" from the fateful moment onwards. This ensures that the act of stupidity that led to the nickname will never be forgotten as the nickname is explained to future generations of staff.

Or the CEO who ranked his group companies on a "pints of beer" scale might have been identified as a Farage-grade pub bore. His staff may then have gone on to notice that the "pub bore" character was backed up by other characteristics such as his tendency to tell the same boring anecdotes on a continuous loop for 20 years. This might well have crystallised into a picture of the man that jaundices the view of many of the staff to this day.

I'm not saying it did happen, just that it might.

But it probably did.

JUST REMEMBER

People who knowingly behave badly have a place in the company's structure as a focus for derision. Their role as a lightning rod for opprobrium gives people a common enemy and stops negativity dispersing itself amongst the team.

People who behave badly but whom you suspect might be genuinely ill should not be ignored and should be treated with sensitivity. If you have one of these, talk to HR and make them work for their money.

TALKING RUBBISH IS A USEFUL SKILL

"It's not that he bites off more than he can chew, but he chews more than bites off."
Clover Adams on the novelist Henry James

If you really want to fit in with the other managers, you will need to master the art of talking rubbish with a straight face. In every meeting, there will be such shameless jargon and round-the-houses talk that you will blush for the perpetrators. Don't bother. They will have learned to live with what they have become, and there will be times when you have no choice but to join their windbagging ranks. These people make pronouncements on things that are so obvious or self-evident that they are hardly worth mentioning, and yet somehow they get credit for it.

In every meeting containing the word "strategy", someone will announce, with the air of a business studies student who has just worked out how to differentiate his arse from his elbow, "What we need to do is to decide where we want to go, what we need to do in order to get there, and how we'll know when we're there." They may follow it up with "So what do we need to do in order to know where we want to go, and when do we need to find out what it is that we need to do?"

You may find yourself slipping into a coma at this point, as your blood flow slows to a sluggish crawl and the bailiffs arrive to take what's left of your will to live.

Sadly, this kind of talk often attracts nods and noises of approval from senior managers. They think that, by agreeing with this nonsense, everyone will believe two vitally important things: first, that the manager deeply understands the situation and second, that they have come up with specific ways of dealing with it that they are just choosing not to mention at that point. In reality, of course, the managers themselves don't have a clue about what to do.

In the summer of 2015, the new chairman of Barclays was quoted in a national newspaper thus: "As a group, if we aspire to bring shareholder returns forward, we need to be much more focused on what is attractive, what we are good at, and where we are good at it."

Having read the newspaper article several times, I still had no idea about exactly how Barclays planned to achieve what were blindingly obvious objectives for any company. If that's what they are prepared to put in a press release, imagine how inane their meetings must be.

If you want to climb onto the next rung of the management ladder, this is a skill that you're going to need to learn. You will need to pronounce this nonsense with conviction and without looking embarrassed. You will need to learn to listen to it from others, and add an extension of your own. You will need to do all of this without developing a deep and lasting self-loathing. Here's a pep talk.

First of all, forget all that stuff about talking only when you've got something to say. "It's better to remain silent and be thought a fool than to open your mouth and prove it" is an hypothesis that has been disproved by many generations of overlooked and underpromoted managers. On the contrary, to make an impact, you need to be seen to be contributing. This means opening your mouth and talking, whether or not you have anything to say.

This cannot be emphasised enough. Unless you make your mark, you will be ignored both at the meeting and outside it. Lurking quietly like a socially inept 16-year-old on the edge of a school disco is not recommended for career progression or, for that matter, for copping off.

If you plan on being too tired or hungover to react quickly to conversation during the meeting, or if you are simply new to the group and lack confidence, then try to turn up at the meeting with a pre-prepared thought or insight. If you can't think of anything, then you have no option but to join in with the others and talk rubbish.

The key to talking rubbish is to talk generically with a straight face and a confident air. Throw in the odd name or process specific to your company to make it look as though you've really thought about it. No-one will be brave enough to challenge you. If they do, repeat what you've just said in a slightly different way with a slightly more frustrated air. At worst, they will think that you're a genius but unable to get your idea across. At best, you'll be seen as someone who really understands what needs to be done – and possibly even have a solution for it, if only your audience were bright enough to understand what it was that you were getting at.

If, at any point, you find that you have exhausted your resources of vagueness, then the best alternative is to go on to blind your fellow meeting participants with meaningless jargon.

A good source of meaningless jargon can be found on social media, particularly Twitter or LinkedIn. Log in and gorge yourself on the vacuous output of your fellow twits. You may even make some friends. Before you know it, you'll be followed by someone whose biography summarises them as "Tech and Biz, Passionate about embedded SW/HW across verticals, Hands-on." I know. I was.

Incidentally, it's always worth checking the comments sections on LinkedIn for sincere-sounding, yet laughably fatuous, arselicking comments that you can appropriate for use when you're in a particularly sarcastic mood. It won't take you long before you find a comment along the lines of this: "Excellent analytic and actionable insight, Darren – wonderful to see your digital chops carry on from our seminal social media days."

Social media can suck up 90% of your available time in its life-wasting aimlessness. But it is also an unending source of drivel for you to delve into and use as inspiration for your contributions to meetings – bearing in mind that your contributions will, from time to time, be totally devoid of meaning. So don't knock it.

If your meeting is so lengthy that you have run out of both vagueness and meaningless jargon, there's still the psychoanalyst technique. You just repeat a point that someone else (preferably your boss) made, as if you've just twigged the cleverness of their thinking. Your sentence structure should be along the lines of this: "So what you're saying is…Ah, that's very interesting." You will then have spoken without committing yourself to anything controversial while also flattering a more senior manager in front of everyone else. Creepy but effective.

To make a real impact, jump up occasionally and write something someone else says on the flipchart (if there is one). Follow up on your surprise physical activity by repeating the comment with a leer of appreciation at the unsuspecting comment maker and an excited look around the room. If nothing else, it will confuse everyone to the point where they think you have just had a blinding flash of insight. While they are trying to work out what it is, sit down again and relax: you have made your presence felt and your job is done.

You can do this. It's easy. You just need to learn to suppress your natural embarrassment at talking such vapid rubbish. Use your competitive spirit to see if you can out-bollocks your colleagues, and gain some satisfaction from that.

JUST REMEMBER

Sitting quietly but attentively in a meeting is not enough. You must find a way to make a contribution – and it doesn't have to be a big one. Just say something often enough for people to notice you're there.

If all else fails, and if you're feeling brave enough, offer to jot down key points from the meeting. That will give you the opportunity to interject occasionally to ask for clarification "so I can get the notes right", hence giving you a role and enabling you to make your presence felt.

UNDERMINING IS BAD
(UNLESS YOU'RE FORCED INTO IT)

"Bette and I are very good friends. There's nothing I wouldn't say to her face. Both of them."
Tallulah Bankhead on Bette Davis

Some people are past masters at the art of undermining others. Whether it's done intentionally or unintentionally, it's not big and it's not clever.

People tend quite naturally to specialise in one undermining technique or other, ranging from the sneaky and conniving to the downright nasty. Learning to recognise and label these techniques is not only important in counteracting their negative effects, but also of vital importance in taking early avoiding action if you are the target.

Here are the main categories of underminer to watch out for.

The hole digger

The clue is in the name. These people dig a hole. Once dug, they thoughtfully guide their target towards said hole, draw their attention to it then, while their victim is looking into it, deliver a helpful shove at the last. Also known as the rug puller.

The flatterer

This is a particularly cynical way of undermining someone. The flatterer latches on to an idea you once had that, they imply, so impressed them that they trot it out with depressing regularity, ostensibly in attempt to curry favour with you. This, far from making you look like a business genius, has the effect of making you look like a one-trick pony. A worn-out old nag who only ever had one idea in the whole of his or her business career. But shutting down the flatterer in front of others looks somehow smug, boorish and ungrateful. This is a particularly nasty form of undermining because it is so disingenuous.

Undermining by flattery goes something like this. "Dave is really brilliant. That round of client lunches we spent twenty grand on a few years ago was all his idea. Even though we didn't get any new customers from it, I don't agree that it was a waste of money. I still think of him as Sir Lunchalot. What a guy!" Or "Becky is great. The paperclip inventory was all her idea. It only took us two months, and the savings very nearly reached double figures. I think of her now as Princess Paperclip."

The politician

The best underminers fall into the "politician" category of staff, unpopular with their team but adored by management; people who may actually want to be a politician. Sneaky and arrogant, the politicians on your team will very likely mask a lack of competence with an almost fanatical grasp of the numbers – numbers to which they themselves have probably barely contributed. Unlike real politicians, they are probably too bright to fiddle their expenses but, in most other respects, they adopt all of the cynicism with little of the altruism that one would like to see in one's public servants.

Politicians are experts at hinting at something that cannot be easily disproved. And even if it is disproved, they never said anything explicitly anyway so they are in the clear. They target victims for no good reason other than some perceived threat. Perhaps the victim is more efficient, more popular or just better looking. This is a state of affairs that, to the politician, cannot be allowed to continue.

The politician's weapon of choice is the implication that the person they have it in for is an employment tribunal waiting to happen.

Let's say that the victim is showing up the politician by taking on more responsibility and getting more work done. You'll be led to believe that the victim is overworked, barely coping and that it will all end nastily. Typical opening shot: "Don't you think that Mike has taken on too much recently? You really don't want *him* signed off with stress."

If the politician is jealous of the victim's popularity, he may try subtly to convince you that the victim is a slacker who spends all their time distracting the rest of your hard-working staff. He may then use employment law to terrify you into believing that the victim is unsackable on the grounds of age, gender, religion, physical or mental frailty, maternity or paternity risk, or sexual preference, leaving you fearing that the victim's next performance review will lead directly to you sobbing in the witness stand at a tribunal, looking like an ageist, sexist racist. Typical comment: "If only Jenny put in as much effort into her job as she does into flirting with the IT guys." Then "Ah well, she's just got married, so she'll be on maternity leave before you know it."

If the politician's nose is out of joint because the victim is better looking, he'll have you believing that the victim is working at the wrong aspect of the job, ie. probably sleeping with one of the management or an important client. Typical comment: "Is it a good idea for X to be spending so much time with Y?" Then, sympathetically, "It must be difficult for you to know what to do for the best." If you know better because you yourself are sleeping with the victim, stop it immediately. That is never, ever a good idea.

Of course, the politician will never say anything directly. But they will leave you in no doubt as to what they are telling you. You will then find yourself linking the unfortunate victim with that familiar gnawing feeling in your stomach, associating them with anxiety and negativity when in all probability they are just getting on perfectly well with their job.

The evil genius

These people know how to implant a prejudice without actually saying anything, thus getting away scot free when the prejudice is proved, usually too late, to be false.

The evil genius may start a conversation with you in quite an innocuous way. Let's say, for example, that you have hired a new manager called Ethel Scroggit who is making the evil genius look like a lazy, talentless oik. The evil genius will at some point say, "What do you make of Ethel Scroggit?" in a tone of voice that leads you to understand that Ethel is being in some way disappointing. The conversation will then play out along the lines of this:

You: "She seems to be getting the hang of it all, doesn't she?"

Evil genius: "Does she?"

You: "Well, she's fitting in well, isn't she?"

Evil genius: "Is she?"

You (by now a little concerned and on the defensive): "Isn't she? What have you heard?"

Evil genius: "Oh, I'm sure it's nothing. Is that the time? I have a meeting. Goodbye."

And there you have it. Complete undermining of a useful newbie in four easy steps.

Some people on their way up believe that undermining a manager at the next level up is a good way of getting noticed. These people really don't deserve to make the grade, not because they are sly but because they are stupid. Undermining a more senior manager is suicidal. They will find out what you have done, they will remember it and they will make you suffer for it. Painfully, and for a long time. So don't do it. And, more importantly, make a note of anyone who does it to you so that you can make them suffer for it later.

If you work with someone who is a natural at undermining, someone who just can't resist doing it, or who has thought up more ways of digging a hole than a Chilean miner, have them "promoted" to the team of someone you hate. And do it fast.

If you yourself are being undermined, the trick is to recognise what's going on early enough to turn it round and undermine the other person using the four easy steps above. It's not big, but you have to admit it is quite clever.

JUST REMEMBER

It's always best to avoid being the sort of person who undermines others. Once you start, it's a difficult – and unpleasant – habit to get out of.

However, if you are being undermined by someone else, then by all means do whatever it takes to protect yourself. If that includes some subtle undermining of the aggressor, then go right ahead. Just remember to stop once you've achieved the desired effect.

WALK LIKE A MAN, TALK LIKE A MANDARIN

"I am sorry to hear you are going to publish a poem. Can't you suppress it?"
Lady Holland to Lord Porchester

Senior civil servants have come to be nicknamed Mandarins. This has nothing to do with the fruit, but everything to do with the impenetrable language and approach they have to their working life. One of their key skills is extreme politeness. Extreme politeness is a skill worth learning. It will stand you in good stead with your bosses and colleagues, and enable you to deal efficiently with any mad old bastards such as non-executive directors or bad-tempered senior managers with whom you have to preserve some kind of civil relationship.

Once, on refusing to play ball with a mad old bastard director who was pressing me to agree to a decision I considered foolhardy for the company, I myself was at the receiving end of the greatest threat he was able to deliver. On hearing that I preferred to attend an important meeting in person rather than just sign over proxy to him, he wrote with the fervent hope that I would not "fall under a bus" on my way to the meeting.

Of course, the opposite was true. There was nothing he would have enjoyed more than a coroner's photograph of four massive Dunlop tyre treads across my finely-honed six-pack. As it was, on my way to the meeting, I developed a bad crick in my neck from looking over my shoulder at busy junctions.

But the point is this. Saying the opposite of what you really mean can make for a very effective way of dealing with difficult people, especially if delivered with lethal politeness. And no-one can pin anything on you. All that the documentation will reflect is your politeness. Nothing can be used out of context because you say nothing at all negative.

The trick to this is in the tone of your voice or email, the use of certain magic words, and the consistency with which you apply them. It goes without saying that your tone should be vaguely – not explicitly – threatening. And there are certain magic words that, when used consistently, signal to your victims that they are in the deepest of deep waters.

To undermine someone's confidence, the word "surprised" is used with depressing predictability by mad old bastards and manipulative geniuses alike. For example, you may receive an email that says something like "I was surprised at your decision to go ahead with the departmental meeting despite the absence of Jonnie Allcock."

You can bet that the surprise was not because they considered the meeting to be any the poorer because of Jonnie Allcock's absence. You know it's because Allcock is their son-in-law and hence their spy in the camp, and so they have gone out of their way to find a way to question your decision, subtly undermine you, and attempt to assert control.

Similarly, when someone is about to blow their top, use of the word "concerned" should be interpreted as something for you to worry about. As in "I was concerned to hear of the lack of progress in the matter". Now you may have had your own reasons for ensuring a lack of progress in the matter. But the fact is that it's been noticed and so you really need to do something. Or, alternatively, anything. It doesn't really matter which.

If someone has been really pissed off by something you've done, they may go for the nuclear option. The nuclear option is "disappointed". Here's an example.

"Dear UK, I was disappointed by your performance in the recent Eurovision".

Translation: "This way to the exit."

Adding the words "most", "very", "highly" or "seriously" in front of the magic words emphasises the danger of the situation to the recipient. But adding the word "awesomely" just makes you look like a dick, so don't do it.

In addition to the magic words, there are magic phrases that have hidden meanings. You need to be aware of these, as people with skills of lethal politeness will often use them as arse coverings, absolving their rear ends of any blame when the shit hits the fan. (Apologies for that analogy – it went further than I had anticipated at the outset.) Here they are, with thanks to www.civilservant.org.uk.

For information: Don't even think of commenting on this, but if anything goes wrong I'll remind everyone you knew what was going on.

I hope this is helpful: I'm well aware that it's not at all helpful. Please go away.

Please do not hesitate to contact me again: Please do not ever contact me again. If you really insist, try in two weeks' time when I am away.

I have reservations about this: If you do this, you're an even bigger idiot than I thought.

I would be interested in your views on this: This is a load of rubbish but as it emanates from a senior director I want you to be the first to say so.

JUST REMEMBER

Even if it means that you have to grit your teeth to snapping point, put on that rictus grin and be as polite as you possibly can be. Consistently. You will win out in the end.

It's a fine line between lethal politeness and sarcasm. Always re-read that key email before you send it, to satisfy yourself that you've kept it on the right side of the line.

YOUR TEAM WILL OCCASIONALLY MAKE YOUR LIFE A LIVING HELL

Razors pain you
Rivers are damp
Acids stain you
And drugs cause cramp.
Guns aren't lawful
Nooses give
Gas smells awful
You might as well live.
Dorothy Parker

At times during your working life, you'll need to protect your sanity from your team's best efforts to destroy it. By "at times" I mean, of course, "most days". You need to hold on to your perspective and humour despite their attempts to rob you of both. Sometimes they really do want to drive you crazy, other times they can't help themselves.

The really cute ones will have mastered the four effective ways of breaking through the façade of professionalism that you are putting on: Obfuscation, Dis-understanding, Prophet of Doom, and Delineation. These are the options that the sanity-busting spirit-sappers are mentally sorting through as they stare at you across the desk.

If you could perfect the skill of mindreading, this is what you would perceive your opponent to be thinking.

Obfuscation

"I'll let you give me my instructions, then I'll give you a detailed run-down on how I'm going to do a slightly different version of what you've asked me to do. I'll go into huge detail about all aspects of this slightly different task: the preparation needed, how I'm going to do it, what the result will be, and what ramifications to expect.

By the time I've finished, you will be frustrated to the point of self-injury and way behind on your own schedule. If you haven't snapped, you will leave me alone for the rest of the day. Guaranteed."

Dis-understanding

"I'll fail to understand something. I'll keep failing to understand while you tie yourself in knots as your explanations and instructions become ever more convoluted or simplistic. I'll ask for more detail on some aspect of the task that you don't want me to do. Finally, I'll say 'let me repeat this back to you so I can check that I've got it', then repeat your instruction but get something wrong."

Prophet of Doom

"I really want you to leave me alone, so I'll concentrate on forecasting disaster at every turn. I know that you are masking a lack of confidence (and competence) with a thin veneer of bravado. So I'm going to give it a light scratch and expose a bit of the sweaty panic and self-doubt writhing underneath.

You know as well as I do that you doubt yourself from time to time – perhaps the decision really *is* bad, perhaps it *will* lead to disaster, perhaps it will cause the fire that burns down your career and everything that goes with it. I'm going to play on this self-doubt until your confidence is shot and you go away."

Delineation

"I will pleasantly point out the boundaries of my job. I'll whip out the job description and long list of core competencies you gave me when I started here and show how I am complying faithfully with every one of them. I'll quickly pick up on any additional responsibilities I'm being required to shoulder and ask if I should perhaps be promoted or at least recompensed for the work I'm doing over and above the boundaries so inflexibly set by the company.

I will leave you with those questions and the fear that you have somehow awakened a dangerous beast. Then I'll look at you in a meaningful way every time you ask me to do something slightly outside my job description. That should do it."

So what can you do when passive-aggressives attack?

Don't indulge them in their pathetic attempt to fluster you. Just reiterate what you want done, when you want it done by and the dire consequences if they screw up.

If you're brave enough, do what an old friend of mine does when challenged by the complaint that "it's not in my job description". He asks the offending party to bring in a copy of his job description. He proceeds to add the task in question to the list of responsibilities, then fixes the offender with a beady eye and says "It is now."

My friend is at pains to point out that you should always follow up such a change in writing, thus: "Thank you for discussing your job description with me today. I am delighted to confirm that cleaning the toilets has been added. I trust it won't be a big job."

Above all, be sure to direct your attention and advice to people who really do want to improve in their job. Prioritise your best people. Ricky Gervais was once asked, in an interview for a magazine, which three things he would save if his house were on fire. His answer was along the lines of "I'd save my photo albums, my passport and…er…one of the twins".

So don't be afraid to prioritise those on your team who are nice to work with and who genuinely want to do a good job. If you need to continually boot someone up the arse to get anything done, they'll end up with a sore arse but you'll go insane.

JUST REMEMBER

People will sniff out weakness in a manager. If you let them get away with this behaviour, *they* will end up controlling *you*.

If you spot anyone indulging in this kind of passive-aggressive or disingenuous behaviour, let the offending employee know that you know full well what they are up to. Then look for an opportunity to offload them. These people never change.

MANAGEMENT IS TEAL AND OTHER NONSENSE

"And thus life in the Oblong Office was a world of secrets and considerations and misdirections, where the nature of truth changed like the colours of the rainbow...But to know what Lord Vetinari knew and exactly *what Lord Vetinari thought would be a psychological impossibility and a wise man would accept that and get on with his filing."*

Terry Pratchett, *Snuff*

As you progress in your career, you will want to develop your own management philosophy. People need to know what you stand for.

You will receive advice on management from many people. Most of it will be unwelcome and/or nonsense.

Just the other day, I was told by an MBA graduate that the basis of management was simply "to tell people what to do and to pay them for doing it". He seemed to think that people could be treated like apps on a smartphone. You, of course, can see the stupidity of this point of view. You will know only too well that the basis of management is manipulation. Manipulation of people and situations by whatever means you have at your disposal to get the result you want.

The same MBA graduate was visibly shocked that I had not heard of some textbook on management which was apparently so important that one could not possibly be a manager without having studied it in detail. When I pointed out that I had been managing people – successfully – for over 20 years, he tried to blind me with theory and jargon to the point where I was forced to remind him that his last company had dispensed with his services shortly after his first and only attempt at managing a team. This is the best way to deal with a Master of Bugger All. Be firm, and find a way to shut them up.

But people continue to try and find new ways of describing management philosophies that make you simultaneously amused and despairing at the pointlessness of it all.

While scrolling through LinkedIn the other day, I saw something so ridiculously ludicrous that I could barely finish my first vodka of the day. What was it that so disturbed my leisurely breakfast? It was a re-posting by an ex-colleague of a new way of classifying management methods.

Setting aside the lack of originality displayed by my ex-colleague in re-posting someone else's work, I wondered what could possibly be so great that he found it necessary to tell his working world about this amazing new thinking. So I clicked on the link, and found a table called "evolutionary breakthroughs in human communication". The author had taken the ways in which humans collaborate and extrapolated them into management approaches. He had then colour coded them for the hard-of-thinking. The result can be summarised as follows:

Teal. Clearly the author's big idea, and the one that will get him on the lecture circuit for life. It's all about promoting self management of individuals instead of a strict company hierarchy. Organisations should be seen as living entities oriented towards achieving their potential. "A few pioneering companies" – those that the writer seems to be sucking up to in the hope that some of their glory will rub off by association – are cited as those from which we should learn important lessons in management.

According to *Wikipedia*, teal is also the colour for wristbands signifying awareness of a long list of nasty conditions, including anxiety disorders and dissociative identity disorder. Feel free to incorporate this into your management philosophy. As one of my fellow managers used to say, "I don't get anxiety. I *give* it".

Orange. These, apparently, are companies that aim for profit and growth in a meritocratic environment. You may think that this is the aim of most companies, including yours, but clearly you would be wrong. Only "orange" companies think like this. This is why you are stuck in your job while the author of this new way of thinking is living the dream on LinkedIn.

Then it all starts getting a little bit out of hand.

Amber. These companies promote formalised roles within a strict hierarchy. The author is a bit sniffy about this approach, but indicates that we can learn from "amber" organisations such as the military and, weirdly, the Catholic church.

Until finally, and hilariously:

Red. These organisations are characterised by a controlling boss who thrives in chaotic environments, a bit like a wolf. There is a constant exercise of power by the boss to keep staff in line. But we can still learn from them. According to the author, organised crime, street gangs and tribal militia are great examples of a "red" approach to management. Using the mafia as a management model is nothing new, but unless you have the weapons and an extended family to back it up, I wouldn't recommend it.

And, in any case, too much intimidation can backfire. Joseph Stalin, the role model for "red" organisations and psychopathic managers everywhere, died after suffering a major stroke, lying paralysed in his bed for 10 hours before help arrived. His staff were too afraid to knock on the door and disturb him in case they got shot. Then, when one of them was brave enough to knock and enter, there was a further delay as his staff argued about which doctor to call, in case they called the wrong one and got shot. We can only hope that the cuddly old dictator appreciated the irony of scaring his staff into paralysis while...well, you get the picture.

There's absolutely nothing wrong with reading about different management styles and approaches. But if you are relying on theory to run your team, you're on a sticky wicket. If you don't yet have the years of hands-on practice that you need, nothing beats a nerve of steel and a poker face for keeping you out of trouble while you build up your practical experience.

Reliance on management theory will make you unbearable to others. There is nothing funnier than an inexperienced manager who thinks he is an expert. This kind of person will make ridiculous reductive statements that have no effect other than to alienate those around him. Statements like "Of course, management is all about power", delivered with a finality of tone that puts paid to any further conversation which might be useful.

What your managers want – and, moreover, what you are paid to do – is to sort stuff out. Efficiently and without getting the company into trouble. The best way to do this is to manipulate people into co-operating by whatever means necessary. How's about that for a ridiculously reductive statement?

As you gain more experience, you will find your own way in management, as in life. Having your own philosophy is great. You need it to set boundaries for your team so that they know what you stand for and what they can get away with. You can even decide on which part of the Rectitude-Eviltude spectrum you want to position yourself. But you really, really don't have to make it into a gimmick.

JUST REMEMBER

As you progress in your career, you will have to develop your own approach to management. People need to know what you stand for.

But don't bang on about your approach to management. Just do what you do consistently, and before you know it you'll have it all under control. Sort of.

NO GOOD DEED GOES UNPUNISHED

"I rang for ice, but this is ridiculous."
Madeline Astor as she was being helped over the rail of the
Titanic

In the early days of a management career, you will be a nice person. You will care about your team; you may even feel a sense of responsibility for their wellbeing at work. You will want to do things for them (not to them – that comes later).

While the intention is laudable and well placed, it is not without risk. That risk involves the thankless consumption of your good deeds by your staff, followed closely by a massive blowback of ingratitude and negativity that no-one could have predicted.

Here are some examples of things that managers have done for their staff which have backfired spectacularly.

Don't, whatever you do, help your team to detox after Christmas. Just last year, a company of my acquaintance decided to introduce "Fitness month" at the beginning of the year, providing free fresh fruit every day during January. When the free fruit stopped at the beginning of February, there was mutiny.

If you manage a small company with offices that overlook Centre Court at Wimbledon or any cricket ground, think very carefully before offering to host a company party during the event. Once you do it, it will be regarded as an annual event. Staff will expect it. The year that you want to do something different, like go away on holiday with your family or have that stint in the Priory that you've been promising yourself for so long, you'd better hope that a reliable senior colleague is at hand to take over.

If you call off the party because you are away, your team will be outraged. They will plead with you to let them host it themselves, accuse you of treating them like children, and fall over themselves to reassure you that they are trustworthy and mature. But, in the words of Celine Dion, you'd better think twice before allowing a junior team access to office premises and alcohol without supervision. Especially when they've got access to Facebook and a few hundred undesirable friends.

So, if you do something once, make it as clear as you possibly can that it is a one-off. You may consider doing it again at some future date, but you are making no promises. Channel any politician you can bear to bring to mind, but try and sound sincere. They say that sincerity is the key to success. If you can fake that, you've got it made.

Most staff are unaware that there is a limit on the amount of money a company can spend on staff entertainment without everyone being taxed to the hilt. Her Majesty's Revenue and Customs sets an annual per head allowance for staff entertainment – about enough for the Christmas party. Exceeding that allowance opens the door to a new tax hell in which the individual is taxed for receiving benefits in kind. So if the company spends too much, each member of staff has to pay tax on company functions they probably haven't even enjoyed that much.

So next time you're being pestered for goodies or under attack for not displaying sufficient largesse, ask your team which they would prefer.

Option A: An orange a day for a year and a higher tax bill.

Option B: Scurvy, but also safety from the clutches of HMRC.

Anyone who would prefer the attentions of the tax authorities really needs to get on Tinder and find someone real to love.

JUST REMEMBER

When you do nice things for your team, make sure they understand the terms and conditions – in particular the time limit.

It is worth reading up on the tax situation for staff entertainment so that you are fully armed when challenged. Or have a chat with someone in your finance department if you can. They have their uses

YOU WILL SPEND A LOT OF TIME BAFFLED

"Why don't you write books people can read?"
Nora Joyce to her husband, James Joyce

In the wonderful world of work, you'll find yourself from time to time faced with a moving mouth that produces a nonstop torrent of gibberish. You recognise the individual words but, when joined together, the words stop making any kind of sense. Perfectly simple sentences will be made so overly complicated that you find your ears and your brain fighting each other to the death as the English language is tortured to breaking point before your very eyes. Or the converse: you'll be left bemused, maybe even slightly patronised, when someone explains something to you so simplistically that you have an upsetting flashback to that day you threw up on your teacher's trousers in primary school.

Let's start with the curse of making things more complicated than they should be. Here's a good example of overcomplexity from those masters of communication, the US Department of Defense [sic]. Halfway down a corridor at the Pentagon used to be a sign that read "This passageway has been rendered inconducive to human traffic for an indefinite period". What they actually meant was "Corridor closed". Why overcomplicate things?

There are usually two reasons behind making something more complicated than it needs to be:

1. The person doesn't understand what's going on, and is covering up his ignorance with a lot of words.

2. The person knows exactly what is going on, but doesn't want you to know.

Here are some real-life examples of Type 1 overcomplexity from people describing their jobs.

"Within my company, I work to ensure that clients optimise the strategic value of their products through a thorough understanding of stakeholder needs and effective communication with key target audiences."

Translation: I try to help my customers sell more stuff.

Or the following, taken from the self-penned biography of a young but exceptionally pompous twit in a remote backwater of advertising. I have corrected the punctuation to make it readable, but other than that the words are his.

"Being satisfied with your work is like scoring your own eye test. It sounds self-righteous, but it's a point of view that keeps me motivated. I've probably worked on every category there is and some things are true for everything. Firstly, the future is

already here. It's just not evenly distributed. Secondly, you will drive behaviour not leverage it. Challenge the value exchange for the consumer and always ask if anyone cares."

Translation: I'm a tosser.

These examples of Type 1 overcomplexity have been produced by people who really don't understand what the heck it is that they are paid to be doing every day. If they knew, they would be able to write it in plain English.

Type 2 overcomplexity looks and sounds very much like Type 1, the big difference being the motive of the perpetrator. Here are a couple of examples, one from the TV programme *The Thick Of It* and one from my office yesterday. See if you can guess which is which. Here goes.

Exhibit A: *"I categorically did not knowingly not tell the truth even though, unknowingly, I might not have done."*

Exhibit B: *"I don't know where that came from, and I wouldn't have thought that she would not also have not found out why it didn't happen."*

Did you guess correctly? Exhibit B is the real-life example. If you find yourself listening to this kind of thing, the bastards are deliberately out to baffle you.

The worlds of art and wine tasting provide fantastic examples of Type 2 impenetrability because they don't want you to know that they don't know jack about nothing.

Films, too, may be made unnecessarily complicated to fill up time and fool both investors and the viewing public into thinking they have got value for money. In *Raiders Of The Lost Ark*, Indiana Jones is hired by the US government to retrieve the Ark of the Lost Covenant before the Nazis find it and give Hitler the honour of opening it. He undertakes a complicated and ultimately pointless journey, at the end of which his actions cause the Ark to be opened prematurely not by Hitler but by some random Nazis who are killed by its immense power.

If Jones had opted for the simple solution and stayed at home, the Ark would have been found by the Nazis, opened by Hitler, and World War II would have been avoided. So Indiana Jones was directly responsible for the Second World War, simply by overcomplication of what could have been a very simple story.

There is an important lesson in all of this. The lesson is that you cannot trust people to convey anything at all accurately. Sometimes they convey nothing at all, but they make an awful lot of fuss about it.

The other side of the overcomplexity coin is, of course oversimplification. When people really want to cover up their lack of grasp of detail, they will often reduce a point of view to a ridiculously oversimplified absurdity. They think that this will make them look pithy and insightful, while avoiding the need to explain their thinking in detail. These idiots tend to be people who know the theory of everything but the practicalities of nothing. MBA graduates, for example.

Examples I have heard just recently are, as you read earlier, "Well, of course, management is all about power. There's nothing more to say." And "The only real aim for a manager is to encourage self-actualisation of their staff." The last thing you want is your staff self-actualising in your office when you're trying to get your blood pressure down to safe levels.

So what do you do when faced with someone who overcomplicates things to the point of brain-burst? Or presents you with such a stupid statement that you wouldn't even trust them to wait until they die before donating their brain to science?

Both can be dealt with in pretty much the same way.

If you're the victim of a verbal overcomplexity, let the perp get it out of their system and completely ignore what they've just said. Then keep on ignoring it. If it's important, they will find a way to make you understand. If the overcomplexity is in writing, hack it to bits with a red pen or in tracked changes. Make them write it over and over again until it finally means something.

Oversimplification can be addressed using a very similar approach. The chances are that the oversimplifier has not really grasped the detail of the pickle they are in, the problem they need to solve, or even the lone thought that is pinging elusively around the walls of their echoing cranium. So, when they make their ridiculous comments, what do you do? That's right. Make them go away and write it down with the instruction to fill 10 pages. When they've finished, you can only hope that they've got anything worth listening to.

JUST REMEMBER

Look for those on your team who have a tendency to overcomplicate or oversimplify things. Are you confident that they understand what they need to be doing?

Expression of complex concepts and issues in a simple way is good. Oversimplification to the point of absurdity is bad.

DEALING WITH IDIOTS IS AN EVERYDAY THING

"Assuming a relatively uniform resonant frequency in a passenger jet, how many cats meowing at what resonant frequency of said jet would be required to 'bring it down'?"
Question from "Brittany" submitted to the science webcomic *xkcd.com*

For those of us who have to work for a living, dealing with idiots is an everyday occurrence. Here are four of the more common idiotic traits you'll find in your colleagues, together with a few handy tips on how to stamp them out before the duty psychiatrist arrives to section you under the Mental Health Act.

In the following scenarios, for ease of reading I have used a unisex "he" to signify the role of the manager, although it's always important to remember that both women and men suffer alike at the hands of their team.

Category 1. Stupid idiots

The worst kind of stupid idiot is the idiot that makes *you* look stupid. These people, while often well meaning, create a fog around themselves that causes accidents for other people. They will say and do things that not only make them look feeble minded but which also reflect badly on your judgment.

For example, one of your well-meaning colleagues may undermine you by remembering some casual but embarrassing comment you once made, possibly while drunk, in a fit of sarcasm, or in a naïve attempt to cheer someone up. They dig it up at the worst possible moment and repeat it in front of more important people, thus reminding others that you said it. Result: you look like an ignoramus.

Or a "hopeless case" colleague may, in one of their futile attempts to impress others, make it sound as though you and they share a really strange opinion. Result: you look like a halfwit. Again.

When this happens, the best way to deal with it is to make light of it with a pithy quip. The quip must be clever enough to show that, while you may indeed be guilty as accused, you are also endowed with self-awareness and a quick wit that makes this slight flaw in your character endearing, perhaps even loveable.

If, on the other hand, it takes you until next week to think up a suitable response, don't worry. You are just like the rest of us. Don't, whatever you do, try and re-engineer the same conversation so that you can use your gem of a quip. And don't say "Sorry, I can't understand what you're saying. I'm wearing a moron filter" unless you are confident that you can't be overheard. If you can't use humour to defuse a stupid comment on the spot, the only other course of action is never to mention it again. It never happened.

Category 2. Indecisive idiots

In the great scheme of things, most decisions are very small. Most of the time it doesn't matter what decision you make, just as long as you make a decision and enable everyone else to make progress. If it's the wrong decision, you can often make another one later to correct your course without anyone noticing that you screwed up. This is a concept that the indecisive idiot fails to grasp as they flip-flop interminably over perfectly straightforward decisions.

When you're cleaving your way smoothly through a to-do list longer and more boring than the Emmerdale omnibus, the paralysis caused by the indecisive idiot is, at best, frustrating. At worst, it is dangerous, causing your well-oiled machine to seize up like a fat old CEO after a 50-metre jog. In any case, failure to decide is totally unnecessary.

In psychology, there is a school of thought that the brain does not reach into itself for any deep experience or knowledge when making a decision. Instead, it quickly improvises decisions, based largely on superficial assessment of the relative merits of the information in front of it at the time. In other words, the brain is an improviser and decisions aren't based on such deep understanding as you may think.

If this is true, which it appears to be, then why agonise over any decision? Especially over the typical day-to-day trivia that keep office life on the move. Your job is to manipulate a decision out of these people. If they don't have an opinion on the matter and/or can't decide which path to take, then just tell them what their opinion is and order them to get moving.

Category 3. Self-deluded idiots

Self-delusion usually accompanies self-importance but never self-awareness. These people think they are popular, irreplaceable and generally the life-support of everyone else in the company. They think they know everything, but they don't.

They don't know how other people see them, do they? Consider that fat old CEO whose beer belly enters the room five minutes before the rest of him. He may know how much money the company is losing but the old salad-dodger doesn't know where the Ryvita is kept, does he?

The self-deluded idiot sees himself as an empire builder when everyone else sees him as a spendthrift loser, sacrificing trusted staff to pay for a series of loss-making ventures. He will, for example, convince himself that everyone is obeying his latest edict: let's say it's an instruction to describe the company as a "cluster of specialised teams". He will not believe that most people in the company (and everyone outside it) are calling it a "clusterfuck of failing businesses". The self-deluded idiot looks in the mirror and sees an intergalactic superoverlord of the business, chief of everything he surveys. You look at him and see a beer gut on stumps.

Category 4. Untrustworthy idiots and "Finance Experts"

As you progress up the management ladder, you will find yourself dealing with "experts" brought into the company by someone on a higher pay grade than you. For example, the big boss may decide to employ an external accountant or "finance expert" to provide independent advice and help the board steer the company through the choppy waters of the business world. This is as good a place as any for a quick word of advice about accountants.

Internal accountants and Finance Directors are generally good people, and usually happy to provide useful information to back up any prejudices you may have. An external finance expert brought into the company as a consultant will be presented as someone who can help the company run better and grow for the future; a shit-hot brain capable of challenging the management with insightful questions and observations from an ostensibly independent party.

But this is disingenuous in the extreme.

These people are the CEO's gimp. They are there solely to back up the CEO's wishes. In that respect, they are on a par with HR. Very often, these people, sometimes with nothing more than a failed attempt at GCSE maths and some spurious accountancy exam behind them, will offer breathtaking opinions on what should be done with – and to – the company. Breathtaking in the sense that you find yourself gasping incoherently at the inanity of their opinion.

At this point, I am going to indulge in a short rant about external "finance experts", so bear with me. Their modus operandi is to make you feel financially inadequate and unsophisticated, even though you have a far better grasp of what is good for the company financially than they do. You understand your business and you have skills of intelligence, observation and reasoning. These are four things they will never have.

Remember, you don't have to get your company into debt simply because an accountant tells you that it's cheap to borrow money. Especially not just after his title has just changed to "Head of Corporate Finance" in the two-bit firm he works for. Incidentally, before hiring a firm of financial consultants, especially if it's a small firm with flashy new Mayfair offices, just do a quick Google search and make sure that one of the partners is not about to get busted for fraud. Just saying.

So the external financial expert is very often another of the chairman's harem of ethically-challenged morons who prostitute their principles for money and the approval of whomever it is that keeps them hired. It is not unheard of for a finance expert to help the CEO force other, more productive people out of the company if their thinking is viewed as too independent for the CEO's liking, for example, or if they somehow displease the person at the top. The really unprincipled accountant will have a lot of unpleasant tricks up his sleeve. He will collude with the CEO behind your back, keep useful information away from you and, when the chips are down, he will undervalue your holding in the company thus making it cheap to dispense with you. They do not automatically deserve your trust – far from it.

Of course, because your company is not their company, they have no real vested interest and so they cannot lose out. Like hedge fund managers, they always make money. At a board meeting some years ago, during which an old colleague of mine was pushed to the brink of a lasting depression by the idiotic advice of the external accountant, the said accountant announced that he had to leave early to take another of his clients "to the undertakers". In other words, he had guided another company to the point of death with his financial wisdom, then given it a nudge over the edge with a final piece of helpful advice. Earning him enough fee to pay for a new Porsche and a holiday home in the Caribbean, as it turned out. Every cloud has a silver lining.

But there is a positive in all of this. Whatever the type of idiot, you are providing a valuable service by looking after them all day. Think of it. If these idiots are at work, they can't be out causing trouble somewhere else. Going to work is a day out for them, and a day off for their family.

JUST REMEMBER

Some people have personality traits and quirks that set your teeth on edge. So what? You don't have to like them; you just need to find a way to work around them.

You can't cure an idiot. You can only grin, bear it and, above all, be patient.

THE UNITED NATIONS OF HELL

"Do nothing."
How HSBC's "Assume nothing" global marketing campaign, conceived in the US, appeared when translated and rolled out in many non-English speaking markets

It's always fun to work with other nationalities if you are a Brit, Aussie or Kiwi. Our American friends in particular cannot tell the difference, and are worryingly easily convinced that you are related to the British (or any) Royal Family if you tell them so. If they think you are British, they are usually very happy to accept what you say at face value, which can be a career saver on so many occasions.

It's hard to believe this far into the 21st Century, but it's a fact that the accent still impresses them, making them willing to believe whatever claptrap you are entertaining them (and yourself) with. They also think that they should be reading between the lines, that you are making points far more subtle and clever than they are picking up. When dealing with colleagues of other nationalities, you can play on this insecurity for your own benefit.

Sometimes you can amuse yourself by understanding more about cultural differences and prejudices than they do. Here's a conversation that happened in a New York lift at the end of last year:

Obnoxious man in lift: "You have an accent. Are you Australian?"

Me: "No. Are you Canadian?"

Exit of victim in an inexplicable huff that I should have confused an American with someone from one of the friendliest countries on the planet.

It's a cliché to say that the UK and US are two nations divided by a common language. There's a vast difference in cultures as well as a total failure on the part of the US to understand proper English idiom. And American ethics make for some unnecessary but entertainingly complex situations.

Some years ago, a well-known US company was developing a product for female sexual dysfunction, a condition which they were doing their best to define. As you can imagine their research for anything to do with "female" and "sexual" threw up a lot of interesting, mainly visual, information. And addition of the word "dysfunction" led them into some pretty specialist areas on the internet.

As a result, a nanny net was introduced to protect the staff and the company from anything unpleasant. But the nanny net was so restrictive that it wouldn't let employees search for a holiday in Scunthorpe, let alone anything to do with the market on which they pinned such high hopes for their new product. Finding a way out of this ethical mire took longer than it did for the product to be developed and launched.

Occasionally, you will be tempted to have a bit of fun with your situation as a lone Brit adrift in a sea of other nationalities. But be aware that this can backfire spectacularly. Here's a personal anecdote.

While working in the US for a large multinational corporation, I was invited (as in ordered) to join a team comprising senior managers from all over the world. I was then forced to complete a "personal profile" for the team's private intranet so that we could all read each other's profiles and get a feel for each other. The first few answers demanded were these:

1. *Your name*. Easy.

2. *Your inspiration*. The example given was along the lines of "My inspiration is my brother, because he's kind, caring and cleans my guttering even though he has terminal cancer".

3. *Your personal style*. The example given was "Classic with a twist" or some such meaningless drivel.

Not being able to take such a waste of time entirely seriously, the answer I submitted was this:

1. *Name* – I reported this accurately.

2. *Inspiration* – Tommy Cooper. Knowing that most of my new colleagues were of a whole range of nationalities, I was confident that this would pass without question, while giving my (British) compatriots a bit of a chuckle. If challenged, I was equally confident that I could justify my

answer with some bollocks about cleverness and sleight of hand, with a quip at the end about not dying on the job.

3. *Personal style* – Brit chic. Whatever the hell that is.

The first team meeting was via global videoconference in New York, London and Tokyo. What happened at the videoconference was not what I had anticipated. First of all, my profile had been selected as the only example of how to start the bonding process with others, for the simple reason that I had mentioned a motorbike. And my photograph came up on screens in three continents, and what it said underneath was this:

1. *Name* – accurately reflected.

2. *Inspiration* – completely omitted from the slide.

3. *Personal style* – Tommy Cooper.

On dark, lonely nights I can still hear the muffled guffaws of the UK contingent, and the words "Glass, bottle…bottle, glass" have developed a whole new cringeworthy association.

Incidentally, they had also changed the answer to another question "What characteristic do you value in your co-workers?" so that it read "Willingness to stand their ground". The answer I had actually given was "Willingness to stand their *round*" – rather more drink-based and certainly less confrontational than the answer that my US counterparts had thought to set down on my behalf.

Of course, we Brits are not without our idiosyncrasies that make us entertaining and often baffling to other nations. Our politeness and reticence can work against us in rooms where the need to talk over other people is the only way to be heard. Our desire to eat dinner at 8pm can bemuse other nations, being either far too early (for our European colleagues) or far too late (in the US). Our capacity for alcohol is viewed with awe by colleagues of other nationalities, except for Australians. But our inability then to get up for 7am breakfast meetings can attract disdain from other, cleaner-living nations.

So, when working for a multinational company, be aware of how you might need to change the way you present yourself to make an impact. Then banish any thoughts that you are somehow pretending not to be yourself, and do it with conviction.

JUST REMEMBER

Working with other nationalities is usually interesting and fun. Don't be afraid to change your behaviour if you need to, so that you fit in.

We all have our own idiosyncrasies. If you poke fun at others, remember to do the same to yourself once in a while.

HOCUM LOCUM – BEING THE OUTSIDER

"On the far side of the moon, I didn't even have to talk to Houston and that was the best part of the flight."
Al Worden, Apollo 15 command module pilot

An interim management position is always a poisoned chalice. It pays well, but it's a hard job to pull off. You, like many people, may one day find yourself in an interim role. Maybe you pressed the self-destruct button in your previous job as your patience pinged apart like a burst balloon; perhaps you engineered a freak accident involving the head of a colleague and a flushing toilet, or possibly you were stretchered out having suffered one too many stilettos between the shoulder blades. Whatever, if you find yourself on a fixed-term contract for any reason, you're now in a whole new circle of hell.

Working as an interim/contractor/locum is a double-edged sword. On the one hand, your hourly rate will be far higher than the people around you – they will know it and make you suffer for it. But what they don't understand is that you're not getting any of the benefits, from pensions to the job security that they so irritatingly take for granted.

They will think you're from another universe. You don't know the right stuff, you don't know how the department or company works, you don't know what the politics are, and you don't know which pub they all go to after work. If they eventually tell you, you are doing something right.

You'll sometimes find it hard to care about the individuals around you, and you'd be right. There's no point in putting in too much emotional investment if you're on a fixed-term contract. And they will probably feel the same way. It's nothing personal. Even if they tell you they don't like you as a person, leaving you to wonder how else you are meant to take it. Rise above it all and be thankful that you're not tied permanently to the hellhole.

Interim roles are meant to have many benefits. This is how you will sell it to yourself and other people. The benefits are these:

Flexibility. That is, flexibility for you to work all hours for a fixed contract. And the flexibility in attitude you'll need when turning up to work every day after the permanent team decide that they can't be bothered to welcome you into the fold.

Self-employment. So others will know that you are not as invested in their company as they are, and hold it against you when you make or support decisions that are not in their interests.

Variety. The variety of people you'll get to meet might cause you to lose all faith in human nature.

Freedom to take holidays whenever you want. And have them realise they can do perfectly well without you.

Learning on the job. That'll make up for the absence of training opportunities then.

Maturing as a professional. You'll have to. Being an interim manager can be a lonely place, and you'll age significantly as you struggle your way through it.

But if it's something you have to do, or have chosen to do, get used to being the Outsider. And make sure you bill them for every minute of torture you endure at their cold, unloving hands.

JUST REMEMBER

Patience and a mature attitude are the key to success as an interim manager. You'll need vast quantities of both.

Don't take it personally if the people around you don't accept you completely into their fold. They are your workmates, not your friends.

BOARD GAMES: WHAT TO EXPECT WHEN YOU'RE ON A SENIOR TEAM

"Maybe you could go and run a tea shop."
Mad old non-executive director to female director (and co-founder) of successful multinational company, c. 2011. Anonymised for obvious reasons (in case the female director ever decides to act on the murderous rage incited by this remark)

If you find yourself in a position where you are on a management team, or have to deal directly with senior management or a Board of Directors, you now have to unlearn any talent for the job you may once have had, stop caring about anyone who reports to you, suppress any sensible plans, and toughen up quick.

Many senior managers and directors are removed from the day-to-day management of the business. They will not know, or will have long forgotten, the knife-edge on which the business teeters.

They will not be tortured by those demons that wake you up at 3am to remind you that you are screwed if your star player finds another job, or scare you into believing you may have pressed "reply all" when forwarding that sarcastic comment about your client. They do not, like you, log into their emails each morning in a state of high anxiety, worried that something has happened overnight to cause the loss of the company's biggest customer and that it's somehow your fault.

Many senior company personnel live in a fool's paradise, cushioned from the knocks of everyday life by an addiction to the company's figures. They assume that the money will keep rolling in, while you are distressingly aware of all of the things that could easily go very, very wrong – literally overnight. They get their thrills from playing games, not playing nice. And they will involve you in their games, whether you like it or not.

Note that, for the rest of this chapter, I use the word chairman and the unisex "he" as shorthand to encompass men and women. At this level, both sexes are equally manipulative and determined to get their way. There is no difference between the determination of men and women in getting what they want, especially once they have reached the top of the tree.

The chairman or whoever is in control will always attempt to ensure that meetings endorse whatever it is he wants to do. This usually involves controlling the agenda, then sorting everything out well beforehand to ensure that the meeting goes his way. This in turn involves getting the most important individual members of the board to agree with him well before the meeting.

If you are a more junior manager or board member, you can forget any dreams you may have of having your voice heard. You are not Henry Fonda in *Twelve Angry Men*, changing the minds of everyone else around the table to pursue the path of fairness and justice. If you speak your mind, fine, as long as it's in line with what the most influential members of the board want.

If you think differently, think carefully about which battles you fight or you will be labelled a troublemaker. The chairman will then deploy a mad old bastard, probably related by blood, marriage or school, to tell you off. These non-executive director types know nothing and/or have a background in investment banking, which is essentially the same thing. The moment you find yourself being told off by an elderly old git with tidemarks round his trousers, start planning your revenge.

It's sad to say but, once on the senior team, constant vigilance is needed if you are to preserve your position. A poor chairman will lobby directors individually behind each other's backs to achieve a result that only he or she wants. If you are in the minority on a team where the other directors are related to each other, be aware that they will sort out what is in their interest behind your back and then do whatever it takes to push it through – with or without your co-operation and very often without your knowledge.

Quite apart from this, subgroups of managers or directors will coalesce to try and push certain items through, then dissolve and re-coalesce in different formations at other meetings. How is it possible to be on the winning side at all times? People need to like you and rate your opinion, but you don't want to form any permanent allegiances that might one day blow up under your ever-growing Pinocchio nose. Be careful not to fight other people's battles for them. If others are going down, let them.

STILL WANT TO BE ON THE SENIOR TEAM?

You should. It's an opportunity to have real influence on the company that you've bust your chops to grow. You'll just need to grow a thicker skin. And it's up to you to make sure you know what is going on and what you are entitled to know. Make sure you see a draft agenda before the meeting, and don't let anyone discourage you from adding any items you want to discuss. If you are appointed to the board of your company, they should provide you with the articles of the company and any other relevant documentation or agreements. The articles should state the rules governing board meetings; how often they will be held, how much notice should be given of meetings and who has what voting rights and other things that you will initially take on trust but which you may later need to question.

You have as much right to sit on the senior team as anyone else (you've been invited, haven't you?). And you are fully entitled to have your voice heard even if your accent, like mine, is not the cut-glass English accent of the 1950s as practised by the mad old bastard non-executive director (see above). These people are not your parents, remember, and you have every right to speak and be heard as an equal.

Above all, be aware of the possibility that things are going on behind your back. Look for trouble, learn to sniff out anything suspicious. If you think you don't know what's going on, ask for the latest documentation. Make it easy for others to tell you things you may not know. But be alert. You cannot be too paranoid.

JUST REMEMBER

Choose which battles you fight at board or management team level. Then, when you've chosen them, do whatever you have to do to win.

Don't form a permanent alliance with anyone or, if you do, be confident it's someone cleverer than you who's going to be sticking around for the long term.

THERE'S ALWAYS A BIGGER FOOL THAN YOU

"Darwin Awards are unlikely to be awarded to individuals who shoot themselves in the head while demonstrating that a gun is unloaded. This occurs too often and is classed as an accident. In contrast, candidates shooting themselves in the head to demonstrate that a gun is loaded may be eligible for a Darwin Award—such as the man who shot himself in the head with a "spy pen" weapon to show his friend that it was real."
Ben Lendrem *et al*, *British Medical Journal*,
December 2014

However badly you think you may have screwed up any given situation at work, take heart from the fact that there is always a bigger fool than you hovering overhead in more senior ranks. The higher up the tree you climb, the more breathtaking the mistakes become. Similarly, the fatter the ego, the bigger the howler.

Managers do stupid things every day. It's hard to imagine, but I myself have committed many howlers – some of them leading to full-blown disasters – but I try to do whatever it takes not to get found out. The great thing about disasters is that it's usually never very long before the next one puts the current crisis into perspective.

If the worst happens and you haven't managed to dodge that bullet, you can absolve yourself of all responsibility using one of the following tried and tested techniques:

1. **It was like that when I found it**. As in "I just followed the system set up by my predecessor". Don't feel bad about this. When you leave, your replacement will do the same to you.

2. **It came off in my hand**. As in "Someone else must have loosened it."

3. **Big boys made me do it**. "I thought you wanted me to do it. I was only obeying orders."

4. **And anyway, I was on holiday at the time**. "Someone else did it when I wasn't around to stop them."

Of course, you could always consider flat-out denial, but this would be a schoolboy/schoolgirl error. The problem then becomes what to do when it all comes out and you have to defend your position. Defending an indefensible position is never a good look. It's a look that can bring your glorious career to a screeching halt because – and there's no easy way of saying this – it makes you look like a nutter.

As a brief aside, a physics professor called Alan Sokal once wrote a completely nonsensical paper and published it in a respected journal to see if they would publish an article full of bollocks if (a) it sounded good and (b) it flattered the editors' ideological preconceptions. Despite the title "Transgressing the Boundaries: Towards a Transformative Hermeneutics of Quantum Gravity" and the premise (that gravity was a social and linguistic construct), the journal not only accepted the paper, but defended it and continued to defend it even after Sokal himself confessed that it was a practical joke.

This is, as you now know, a silly course of action by the journal when it had at least two totally believable excuses at hand. Having been found out, the journal editor should, of course, have used excuse number 4 and claimed to have been on holiday at the time the paper was accepted for publication. His staff should have been told to use excuse 3 (that they thought they were expected to publish it), thus making it all look like a big misunderstanding. What are we like!

While, in most companies, stupid actions don't reach the stratospheric proportions of the Darwin awards, they are still pretty stupid. The Darwin awards, as everyone knows, recognise people who contribute to evolution by self-selecting themselves out of the gene pool through putting themselves at unnecessary risk in life-threatening situations.

Here are some classics against which to measure the stupidity of your bosses or colleagues:
- Juggling live hand grenades (Croatia, 2001)
- Leaving a lit cigarette in a warehouse full of explosives (Philippines, 1999)

- Accidentally blowing yourself up with your own bomb set on daylight saving time, one hour ahead of local time (Israel, 1999)
- Jumping out of a plane to film skydivers without wearing a parachute (US, 1987)
- Using a lighter to illuminate a fuel tank to make sure it contains nothing flammable (Brazil, 2003)
- Attempting to play Russian roulette with a semi-automatic pistol designed to load the next round into the chamber automatically (US, 2000)
- Crashing through a window and falling to your death while trying to demonstrate that the window was unbreakable (Canada, 1996)
- Making the fourth of July that little bit more memorable by launching an extra-large firework from your own head (US, 2015)

Some people are spectacularly inept, and deserving of a whole new category of professional Darwin awards: for people who remove themselves from their own jobs due to breathtaking arrogance or stupidity.

Take, for example, the manager who ordered his team to negotiate a substantial discount with one of their suppliers. Having just got the suppliers to agree to knock 30% off their prices after a few hours' tough talk, the team were aghast to see their manager breeze into the meeting room, tear up a random piece of paper, and say "You need to give us a 20% discount or we take away our business. Take it or leave it." The delighted supplier took it. The manager swept out of the room with a triumphant: "And *that's* how it's done."

And a story I heard just last night from a designer who had been called to a meeting and unexpectedly "offed" on the grounds that, as there was a dwindling need for print buying at the company, his role was therefore redundant. With great presence of mind, he whipped out his job description and pointed out that nowhere in it were the words "print buying" mentioned. He rammed home his point with the observation that "I don't think you can get rid of me due to a dwindling need for something I'm not supposed to be doing" and an innocent comment about asking his solicitor about it all. A red-faced MD and his HR henchwoman ended up forking out the best part of a year's salary rather than the statutory redundancy they had forecast. And all because they were too stupid to check a basic fact.

Now draw yourself an axis of stupid, with "not especially stupid" at one end and "Darwin awardwinner" at the other. Every time you commit a howler, mark it on your axis of stupid. Now do the same for your boss or any colleague you'd like to get even with.

You're not so bad, are you?

JUST REMEMBER

Head off trouble by planning for the worst-case scenario at all times. One day it will happen, and you will look like Mystic Meg.

Try not to do anything too stupid but, if the worst happens, stay calm. One of your colleagues or bosses will undoubtedly have done something much worse over the course of their career.

COMING TO TERMS WITH YOUR DESTINY

*"Life is always either a tightrope or a feather bed.
Give me the tightrope."*
Edith Wharton

A seasoned manager will have long forgotten the principles with which she (or he) first enthusiastically embraced the challenge of staff management. They will also know that people who profess enthusiasm for management have either never done it or are barefaced liars. These people are not your friends. Look in the mirror and say it 10 times before you leave for work in the morning, then repeat as necessary as the day wears on.

People seek comfort from the challenges of management in a variety of different ways – excessive exercise, sex with the wrong people, psychotherapy, drink – and all are perfectly valid strategies. To paraphrase Homer Simpson, "Alcohol – the cause of so many of the world's problems, but the answer to all of them". Substitute "alcohol" with "sex with the wrong people", and you'll see how much potential you have.

The trick to surviving in management is to come to terms with the fact that the best you can hope for is to preserve fairness in the way you approach your charges. You are neither their parent nor their friend. You don't even need to particularly like someone, as long as you can find a way to work with them. And they don't necessarily need to like you. An uneasy truce is the modus operandi in more companies and teams than will ever admit to it. Anything more than that is a bonus.

In case you're wondering, I successfully exited a company that I set up and ran for many years and I am still in touch with many of the staff there. They send me photos of themselves and their children, befriend me on Facebook and, from time to time, invite me to the pub after work. I am still at large, working now for fun, and practising the dark arts on a new generation of victims.

If I had to pick out one single fact of life to pass on to my fellow managers, it would be this. Nobody is indispensable. When you leave your job for another, as one day you will, there will be no widespread wailing and gnashing of teeth however popular you think you were. On the contrary, your old team and bosses will not bat an eyelid. They will view your departure in these simple terms:

that they haven't so much lost a colleague as gained an office.

So keep things in perspective in your working life. If people like your schtick, they'll buy it. If they don't like it, and if that makes you unhappy, then move on to somewhere that appreciates the way you do things.

I hope that this book will have shown you some of the more effective management tactics that will help you negotiate the management minefield. Of course, you will want to develop your own tactics as you yourself gain different experiences. There is no such thing as a model manager: you will develop your own style and that style will be just as valid as anyone else's.

You will certainly have good times and bad; times when you feel on top of your game on the occasions when your team is managing to pull together under your control, and times when you will feel powerless and manipulated by your own staff. This is par for the course. An experienced manager will ride the bad times and profit from the good.

Just remember: even if the faces you see every day become as familiar as your own, even if you spend more time with them than you do with your family, and even if you catch yourself feeling the odd stab of affection for them from time to time, these people are not your friends.

10 WAYS TO REALLY SCREW UP AS A MANAGER

If, after all of this, you are still determined to screw up, then here's how.

1. Don't have your own office. Sit in an open-plan area in as public a spot as you can. That way you can avoid all of those pesky private conversations with people who just want to sort things out.

2. Communicate only by email. Talking is dangerous. If you're not sure you're going to be able to win a conversation, don't have it.

3. Always work through other people. Manipulating people to act against others makes them complicit in your plans. They become both increasingly unpopular and increasingly dependent on you (no-one else will want to talk to them). And you look like the good guy.

4. Manage by "hint". Never be explicit in what you want. Make people feel clever at having "got" your hint. Then, later on, deny that you meant anything by it. This is the best way of engendering paranoia among the sanest of individuals.

5. Pick your favourite people in the team and make it clear to everyone who your favourites are.

6. Be as self-important as you can manage without repulsing yourself unacceptably. Then deal with all problems in as heavy-handed a way as you can think of. Use a sledgehammer to crack a nut at all times.

7. Never nip anything in the bud. Escalate it.

8. Ignore potentially difficult situations until they *are* difficult, then discipline someone.

9. Prevent other people from messing things up by excluding them from decision making.

10. If someone disagrees with you, ignore it and keep ignoring it until the issues (or they) go away.

SIX BOOKS TO READ OVER A STIFF DRINK

Each time you achieve a small victory on behalf of your team against your own management, award yourself an hour with a litre bottle of strong alcohol of your choice. Alternatively, spend your leisure time more constructively by reading some of these books and thinking laterally.

Nick Lane. *Life Ascending.* 2009; Profile Books. A wonderful account of the 10 great inventions of evolution. Fascinating in its own right but also useful, with a bit of imagination, for inspiring thoughts on evolving your own team.

Dashiell Hammett. *The Maltese Falcon.* 1930; various publishers. A masterclass in deception and duplicity.

Tom Peters. *The Pursuit of Wow!* 1994; Random House. Tips on how to manage your team and your own career from someone who has clearly never worked as a manager in the UK.

Thomas Paine. *Common Sense.* 1776; various publishers. How to put forward a well-reasoned argument at length.

Terry Pratchett. *Snuff.* 2011; Doubleday/Corgi Books. Or any Terry Pratchett book that includes Lord Vetinari, ultimate manipulator and control freak.

PG Wodehouse. *The Code of the Woosters.* 1938; various publishers. In which Bertie is made by his Aunt to go to an antiques shop and "sneer at a cow creamer" in order to sap the owner's confidence and drive the price down. Make of this what you will.

ACKNOWLEDGEMENTS

The idea for this book is over 10 years old. I should have written it long ago, but I have been far too busy trying to be the model manager. Reassuringly, the past decade has only proved that some things never change – they only get more so.

I selected for inclusion several of the management tricks that I have found most useful over the years, together with some more sinister activity by colleagues. These tricks and observations have helped me stay relatively sane, and are illustrated by (mainly) real-life examples. While some of the anecdotes involving named famous people may be apocryphal, the anonymised stories are not. Names and details of specific companies have been removed in an attempt to avoid legal action but all are true. I know they are true because I was there.

Several people were instrumental in making this book what it is. So, to Sarah, John, Ana and Nick…this is all your fault.

ABOUT THE AUTHOR

Jason Lye is a pseudonym behind which the author, an inveterate coward, is hiding. The author has a 23-year history of management at all levels in companies of all sizes. He hopes to while away his remaining useful years picking up tips for management bestsellers that will entertain him and others like him, as they bravely face the daily battering of office life.

THESE PEOPLE ARE NOT YOUR FRIENDS

THESE PEOPLE ARE NOT YOUR FRIENDS

JASON LYE

Printed in Great Britain
by Amazon